guide to PATTERN & COLOR

Decorating ideas for your home

CREATIVE PUBLISHING international

Minnetonka, Minnesota

Table *of* Contents

Pattern Plays

Elements of Color & Pattern

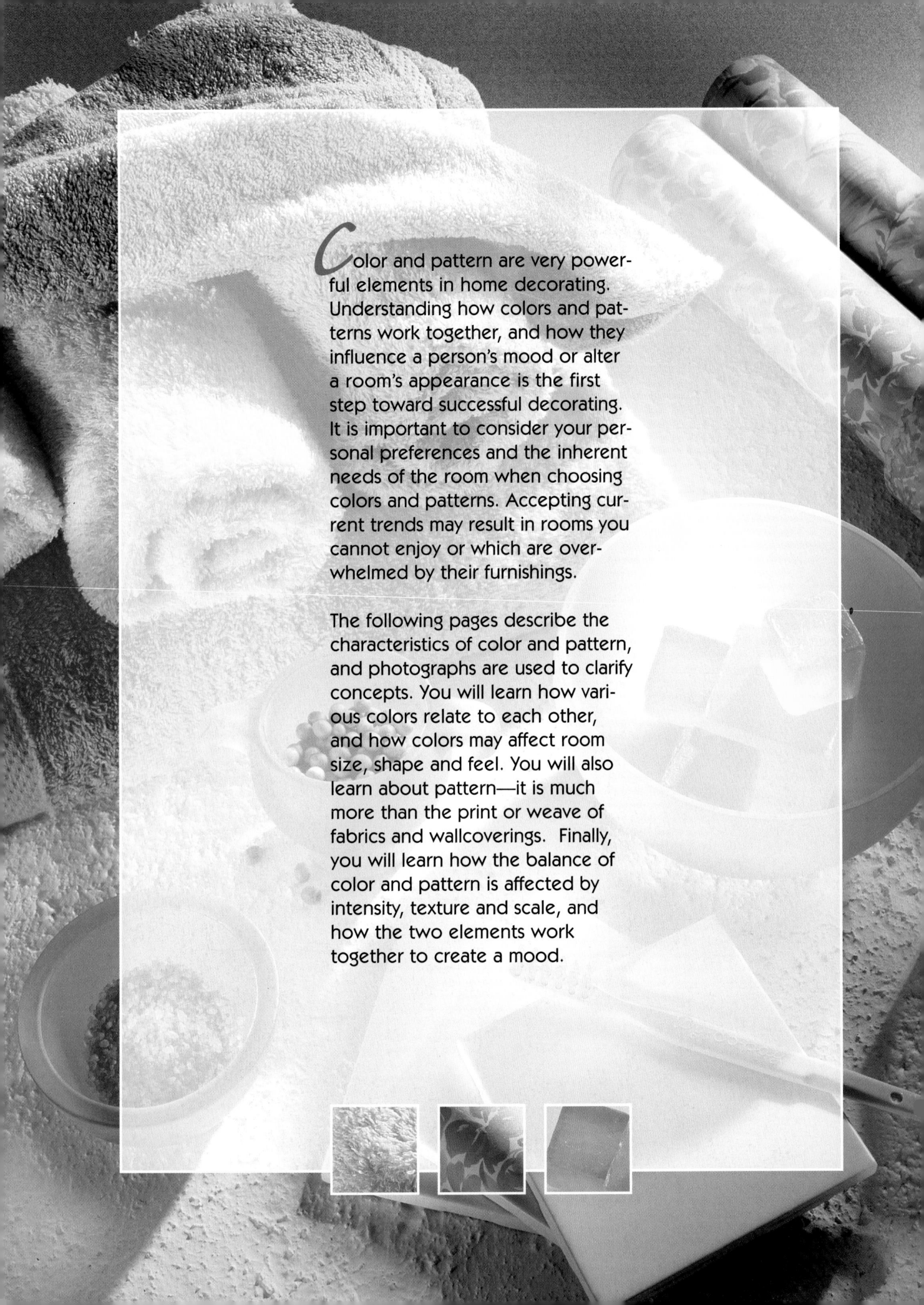

Color and pattern are very powerful elements in home decorating. Understanding how colors and patterns work together, and how they influence a person's mood or alter a room's appearance is the first step toward successful decorating. It is important to consider your personal preferences and the inherent needs of the room when choosing colors and patterns. Accepting current trends may result in rooms you cannot enjoy or which are overwhelmed by their furnishings.

The following pages describe the characteristics of color and pattern, and photographs are used to clarify concepts. You will learn how various colors relate to each other, and how colors may affect room size, shape and feel. You will also learn about pattern—it is much more than the print or weave of fabrics and wallcoverings. Finally, you will learn how the balance of color and pattern is affected by intensity, texture and scale, and how the two elements work together to create a mood.

UNDERSTANDING COLOR

If you have ever wondered why some color schemes are more successful than others, consult the color wheel for clues. This visual tool shows you at a glance how colors relate to one another.

A change of color scheme is the quickest way to alter the appearance of a room, to give it anything from a fresh new look to a radical change of style. Whether you are starting from scratch or incorporating existing features into the scheme, choosing colors you like and feel at ease with should always be a priority. Color preferences tend to be instinctive – many people naturally prefer the 'warmer' shades of red, yellow and orange, while others opt for the 'cooler' blues and greens. These different qualities are invaluable decorating tools.

Warm and cool colors

You can use the invigorating effect of warm colors in living rooms and busy areas and, as warm colors tend to make a space appear cozier, they can effectively 'pull' a room together. Cool colors create quite a different effect: they have a calming quality and tend to recede, making a room seem larger and airier. When you combine warm and cool colors in varying amounts you create a visually interesting, subtle balancing act – and achieving the right color balance is the base for any successful scheme.

▶ *Refer to the color wheel to help you choose color schemes to suit your home.*

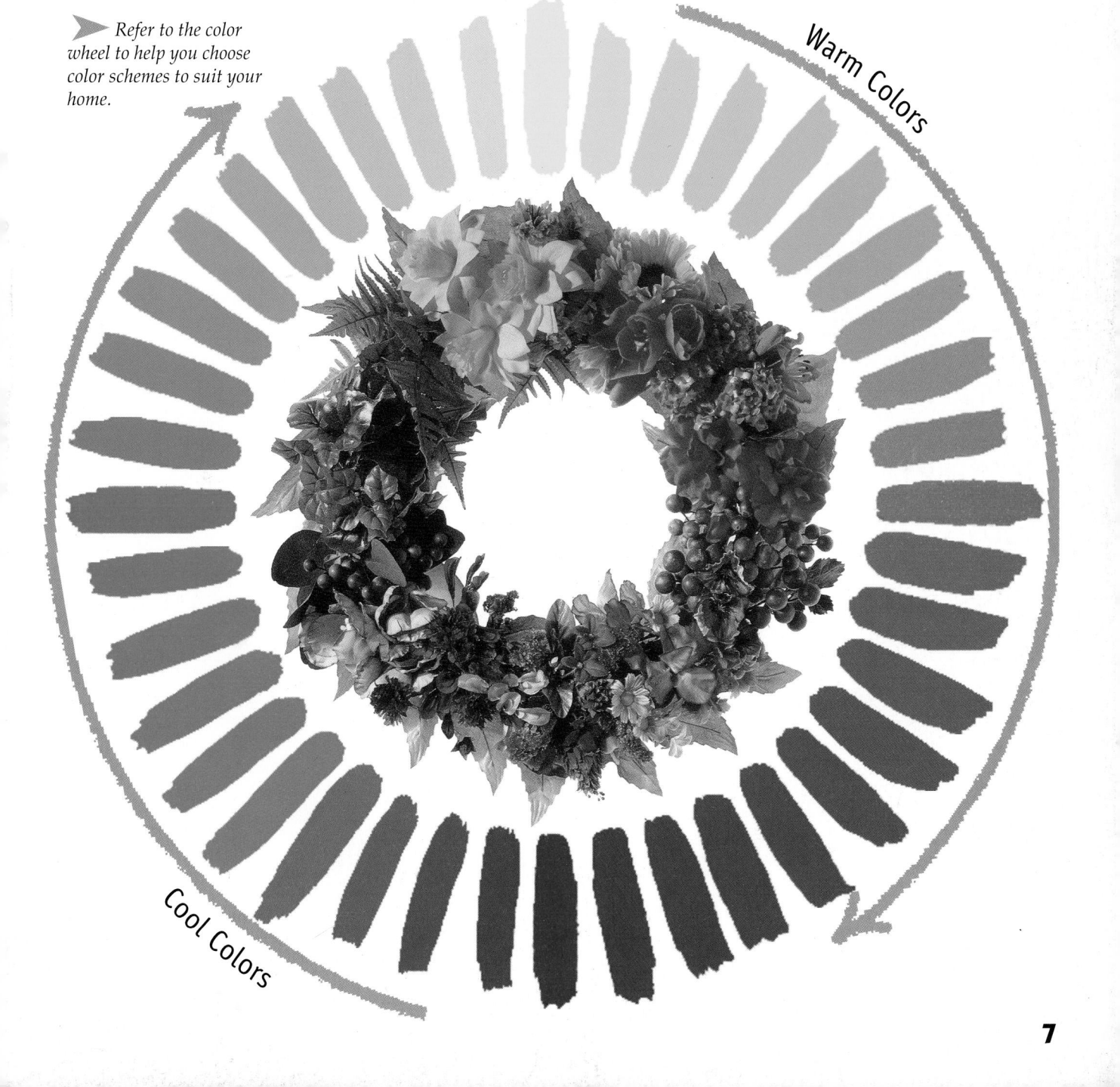

Warm Colors

Cool Colors

Explaining the color wheel

Seeing how colors are positioned on the color wheel, and recognizing the terms used to describe their relationships, will be a great help to you when planning your own color schemes. The color wheel divides in half naturally, with the warm, advancing colors, such as the reds and oranges, on one side and the cooler, receding greens and blues on the other side. These pure colors are mostly too bold to use full strength for decorating, except in very small amounts. Consequently, schemes are based on colors reduced in intensity by the addition of black, white or gray.

The qualities of color and the expressions used to describe them in decorating terms are defined as follows:

Hues The pure colors on the wheel are called hues.

Tonal value By adding varying amounts of white or black to reduce a color's intensity you alter its tonal value.

Tints Colors with white added are called tints, or pastels.

Shades Colors with black added are called shades. In decorating, muted tones of pale tints and shades are mostly used to create color schemes.

Primary colors Red, yellow and blue.

Secondary colors Orange, green and violet. These are made by blending the primaries: red and yellow make orange, yellow and blue make green and blue and red make violet.

Tertiary colors Yellow-green, blue-green, yellow-orange, red-orange, red-violet and blue-violet. These are made when a primary is mixed with an adjacent secondary color.

Neutrals Black, white and gray, which do not appear on the color wheel, are true neutral colors. For decorating purposes, soft browns, taupe, beige, mushroom, gray tints and cream are also called neutrals.

Harmonious schemes are based on hues, or pure colors, which sit together between two primary colors on the color wheel.

Complementary and contrast schemes put colors together from different sides of the color wheel, by balancing a warm color with its cool opposite. True complementaries such as red and green, blue and orange, and red-orange and blue-green, lie directly opposite each other on the color wheel. Contrasting, or split-complementary colors describe those hues not so precisely positioned on the wheel, but which retain the warm/cool balance.

Monochrome schemes, also called one-color schemes, are based on variations in tone and intensity of a single color.

Warm cools/Cool warms Some colors, though predominantly cool or warm, may have a hint of color, which makes them appear as warm cools or cool warms. Similarly, a hint of color may warm or cool neutrals.

HARMONIOUS SCHEMES

Colors that blend into one another on the color wheel always work together pleasingly, so any color scheme worked in this limited way is easy on the eye. This approach can sometimes look a little one-dimensional, but by introducing a few accessories in an accent color from farther away on the color wheel, you can give the scheme more life.

Adjacent harmony schemes

Adjacent schemes are based on groups of colors that lie next to each other on the color wheel or from groups of colors taken from three or four adjacent sections. Harmonious schemes using colors placed each side of a primary color, such as yellow-green, yellow and yellow-orange, are naturally more discordant, and they need careful handling to work well.

You can combine warm and cool hues successfully, perhaps using a group of warm colors for the main theme, with cool accents for visual interest, or as a cool scheme with warm accents. When using warm and cool colors in equal amounts, you can balance the effect with neutral accents.

▼ Warm harmonies

Hot spice colors and warm earth tones create a richly glowing scheme in this sitting room, where the colors and textures are used in a dramatic way. The large expanse of plain, burnt-orange carpet acts as a subtle foil for the stripe theme echoed in the walls, curtains and the metal lines of the furniture.

▲ Cool harmonies

The cool side of the color wheel inspires the fresh aquas and restful blues in this bedroom. Chalky tints used as the base for the scheme are boosted by touches of stronger blue and green. This combination is shown to advantage by a liberal dash of white and neutral details.

► Adjacent harmonies

This bold yet muted scheme shows how colors taken from each side of a primary color can inject a real feeling of vitality into a room. Here, the pale green, stronger toned green and warm terra-cotta create a subtle balancing act with the yellow walls.

CONTRAST SCHEMES

Colors on opposite sides of the color wheel always bring out the best in one another and help to create a vibrant environment. Used in equal quantities, true complementaries are too overwhelming for most schemes, but toned-down versions of these colors, either mixed with white to soften them, or muted with a touch of black, work together beautifully.

Pink and pale green is a favourite variation of complementary red and green. Paler tints of blue and yellow, and violet and yellow-green are also popular combinations.

Color contrasts are achieved by shifting round the color wheel slightly to match hues; as opposites, violet and yellow-green are complementaries, but violet and green are color contrasts, as are blue and red-orange.

A tried and tested way to create contrast color schemes is to use an expanse of a cool, receding color balanced by smaller amounts of a warm color. Contrast colors also work well used in a subtle way, teamed with white or set against a neutral background. They are also effective when introduced to harmonious schemes as color accents.

◢ Contrasts and complementaries

On a red and green theme, pink and lime are soft contrasts, while the stronger touches of red and green are broken with white to lighten their effect. A neutral carpet provides a cohesive background for the fragmented splashes of color and pattern.

Contrasting tints

Lashings of white reduce yellow to a relaxing, almost neutral tint in this sitting room. Soft furnishings and pattern details in stronger tones of yellow and contrasting blue add interest without compromising the restful atmosphere.

Color accents

A generous sweep of warm yellow only needs a touch of cool marine blue to balance its impact. An added twist of red creates a triatic color scheme of primary hues, and provides a lively mid-tone accent between the yellow and blue.

MONOCHROME SCHEMES

Monochromatic, or single-color, schemes are the easiest to create. Ideally the tonal mix should include pale, mid and deep tone highlights to create the right balance, and to prevent the scheme from looking flat and dull.

Besides using variations of a strong color, monochromatic schemes can also be based on warm or cool neutrals, such as teaming white, beige and taupe with natural materials.

▶ Pink and more pink
The success of this scheme owes much to the strength of the various pinks, which look charming, rather than sugary-sweet. White acts as a foil for the mid pink walls and the stronger toned bed cover and the curtains.

▼ Cool minty greens
Here, varying strengths of peppermint green are balanced against a cool white background. The fresh green mid tones in the curtains reappear in the antique washstand, whose curves echo the lines in the fabric design. Touches of refreshing white create a visual link throughout.

▲ Lavender blue
A colorwash of warm lavender blue provides a mid-tone background for the paler soft furnishings. A cushion in deep lavender reinforces the single color theme, and a heathery pink throw adds a harmonious color accent.

PLANNING FOR COLOR

The first steps in planning a color scheme for a room are to consider important details such as your likes and lifestyle as well as the merits and drawbacks of the room itself.

Your first considerations when choosing a color scheme are likely to be based on your personal preferences, a favorite room seen in a magazine or the latest fabrics and wallcoverings on sale. However, to make the most of a room, first think about the room itself and how you intend to use it. Aim to reach a scheme that caters to all your needs, activities, tastes and budget, while playing up the room's good points and also taking into account existing furnishing items.

Identify the positive aspects of the room and work to enhance or emphasize these. At the same time, think about disguising or drawing attention away from any bad points, rather than simply ignoring them.

On the following pages, a checklist guides you through all the aspects you need to consider when planning a color scheme. Look at the form and function of the room; the amount of natural light it receives or provision for artificial light; any existing problem features or any furnishings that

can't be changed. Then begin to build up a summary. Apply your answers to any later decisions you need to make about choosing a color, pattern or room style.

▼ *A striking marbled fireplace can be the perfect starting point for a color scheme. The welcoming peachy glow of the walls in this sitting room has been matched carefully to the color in the marbling, and echoed again in the chair fabric and lamp shade.*

ROOM CHECKLIST

Work through the questions that follow. Make detailed notes of your answers so that you can analyze how they relate to one another and what your priorities are.

SIZE AND SHAPE

- Is the room large or small?
- Is the room long and narrow or boxy?
- Are the ceilings low or high?

Colors and patterns can work visual magic on architectural imperfections. In a small room, you can increase the sense of space by using pale colors that reflect the light to give a more airy feel. Darker tones and warmer colors have the opposite effect, helping to create intimacy in a larger room.

Patterns are just as useful. In a small room, you can visually stretch the height of the walls using striped wallpaper. Checks, trellis and small repeating patterns have a similar expanding effect.

Using colors and patterns to make the most of a room's size and shape will be covered in more detail in later chapters of this book.

Large rooms can accommodate strong, rich colors happily. Here, the earth tones of terra-cotta walls, brick-colored carpet and soft brown sofa visually add warmth to the room.

Delicate colors and shadow stripes stretch the dimensions of this little room. Cool greens and blues create a fresh, airy atmosphere, and the vertical lines in the wallpaper lead the eye upward to a dainty border defining the ceiling line.

FUNCTION
- How will the room be used?
- Who will use it and how often?
- Does it have a dual function?

You're far more likely to come up with some practical solutions for decorating a room when you take into consideration the role – or roles – it plays in the household. Pale colors are often suited to a room in constant use; for example, a warm buttermilk yellow invokes a friendly atmosphere in a kitchen or family room; or cool greens and blues freshen up a bathroom.

A guest bedroom should be warm and welcoming, but you can be adventurous with strong colors and zany ideas because nobody has to live with them for very long. Likewise, a separate bath, despite its small size, can provide an opportunity for colorful escapism.

In a dining room, restricted mainly to evening entertainment, you can use color to establish the atmosphere – with darker colors and ornate window drapes that create an elegant setting.

A dining room which gets most use in the evening can be decorated with an eye for the dramatic – something that will show up at its best with low, romantic lamps or candlelight. Deep colors make the walls seem closer, giving a sense of intimacy, ideal for special occasions.

Color can be the vital key to linking the different areas of a multifunction room. Here, a modern floral fabric brings together the restful blues of the seating area and the greens of the dining area, set against a cheerful yellow background.

15

Light

- Does the room face north, south, east or west?
- Is the window small or large?
- Is there adequate lighting?
- Do you need to block out strong light?

The aspect of a room affects the type of light it receives. In the northern hemisphere, a north-facing room gets a cold, clear light, but if it faces south, it gets sunlight during most of the day. In the southern hemisphere, the reverse is true – a south-facing room gets the cold light and a north-facing one is sunny.

Color changes dramatically under different lighting situations. If a room is used throughout the day, look at the color under all lighting conditions or, if it is only used at a particular time, look at it then. Natural light has a blue cast at midday, but has a warm orange tint towards the beginning and end of the day.

Artificial lighting generally has a yellow cast, although the choice of bulb and shade can change its tint. There are many types of artificial lighting available, and you can use these to create atmosphere as well as for practical purposes.

Unless the window treatment or an external feature blocks the light, a room with large windows will be

Warm up a cool, clear light as it enters the room by framing the window with rich colors and textures. The heavily draped curtains and raspberry-striped blind counteract the effect of the cool greens outside the window.

more affected by natural than artificial light. Decide whether you want to maximize the natural light for a bright, airy feel; screen out dazzling sunlight to create a diffuse glow; or use artificial lighting for a softer, cosier atmosphere. To this end you can also use pale colors that reflect the light and darker colors that absorb it.

For a bedroom, think about screening for privacy and shutting out light while you sleep.

The artificial light from these candle lamps emphasizes the vertical stripes and rich color of the wallpaper, and casts a warm, welcoming glow on an elegant hallway table.

PROBLEM FEATURES

- Is the room an odd shape?
- Are there any ugly features?
- Does the room have a sloping ceiling?

Color can't provide the answers to every problem in a room, but you may be able to use it to visually alter the proportions of an odd-shaped room or to help disguise or detract from an ugly feature.

In a narrow room you can reduce the corridor effect by using a warm color on the far wall, to draw it visually inward. If you have a very small box room you can use color in different ways – either add interest by painting the walls in different colors or acknowledge its simplicity with a minimalist white-out.

To ensure an alcove does not become a pokey corner, either use a pale color that visually opens it up, or use a contrast color that defines the area for a particular function – a study corner, for instance.

Blend in unsightly features, such as pipework or an odd-shaped ceiling, by painting them the same color as the background or surrounding surfaces. Alternatively, you can box in pipework to make a practical storage unit, then highlight it with a strong color to make a feature out of a drawback. To draw attention away from an ugly fireplace or view, use a stronger color or an interesting pattern on the opposite wall.

▲ *The airy stripes of the wallpaper help to play down a difficult ceiling corner formed by the eaves of the house. The pale vertical lines make the most of the height and size of the room.*

▼ *Attic conversions can be awkward areas to decorate. A single color used all over makes all the surfaces flow gently into one another, integrating the ceiling and walls to give a sense of space.*

FIXED ITEMS

- What furnishing items have to stay in the room?
- Are there any built-in features?

When rethinking the look of a room, it is very seldom that you can start from scratch. You usually have items you can't or don't want to change – a fairly new sofa, for example, or coordinating window drapes and bed linen. Flooring is often the last item to wear out, so you may also have to incorporate the existing carpet.

Such *in situ* items may be the starting point for choosing a color scheme. You can often build the scheme around them, taking one or two favorite colors from the pattern and using them in blocks of solid color.

Revamp existing tongue-and-groove boarding in a bathroom by stripping off all the old varnish and choosing a light, unusual color combination like this pretty pale turquoise and lemon.

Good quality soft furnishings are expensive items to replace. However, you can give existing soft furnishings in rich, traditional patterns, like this curtain and headboard fabric, a new lease on life by setting them against blocks of plain, clear color and brisk checks.

CONCLUSION

When you have answered all the questions, you will be able to build up a summary of your ideas about the room. Each of your answers can influence your choice of color and/or pattern, which in turn may suggest a style for the room. The combination of demands that the room and the people using it dictate will guide you toward the most practical, functional and pleasing way of decorating it.

You will be able to use this information to compile a mood board that gives you a basic feel for the look of the room; and subsequently a sample board, filled with swatches of your chosen fabric, paper and paint. Such meticulous preparation pays handsome dividends as you eventually arrive at a tailor-made color scheme and room style.

PATTERN AND TEXTURE

Whether your decorating tastes are for clean-lined, uncluttered looks or something more sumptuous, pattern and texture, together with color and tone, are the most important elements in interior design.

Used successfully in a scheme, the inseparable constants, pattern and texture, complement each other. They provide a pleasing visual and tactile setting, balancing bold lines with intricate details; rough and smooth; matt and shiny; hard and soft. A quick look around you will show how everything in our environment, both in the natural world and in our own homes, combines pattern and texture.

In your home, some 'background' patterns and textures are so subtle that you may overlook them, yet they play an integral part in decorating schemes. In addition to the hard and soft contrasts that occur naturally between walls, carpets and furnishings, there are patterns formed by the grain lines and swirls in wood, the gridlike format of tiles, wood block floors and window panes. These all contribute their own character to a scheme, as do more incidental patterns such as plates on a dresser, rows of books in a bookcase and groups of pictures or ornaments.

Spicy colors set the scene in a harmonious scheme where every surface delights the eye. Patterns and textures echo one another throughout the room, from the formal placing of the furniture and accessories, which create their own subtle patterns, to the curving lines of the bobble-trimmed curtains and gilt bead details on the wall sconce.

Being aware of the interplay between all these elements means you can make the most of their potential in new or existing decorative schemes.

CREATING A BALANCE

A well-balanced scheme incorporates a satisfying mix of pattern and texture, whether the effect is boldly defined or more subtle. Most rooms naturally contain surfaces with qualities such as matte, glossy, rough, smooth, and hard and soft, which you can harness as starting points in a scheme. Fabrics, wall- and floorcoverings are primary considerations after shape, light and color preferences, whether you are creating a special ambience and mood, or a practical, comfortable setting for everyday living.

Room function also has a marked effect on pattern and texture choice, as a quick check in your home will show. Living rooms tend to be warm and comfortable-looking, with fabrics and decorative materials chosen in colors, patterns and textures that reinforce this feeling. Likewise, bedrooms are for relaxing, so bold, vibrant patterns and cold, shiny surfaces seem inappropriate. Kitchens and bathrooms need practical, easy-to-clean surfaces, so smooth, streamlining materials tend to predominate: glossy tiles, smooth laminates, shiny metals and glass lend themselves naturally here.

These accepted groupings of pattern and texture can be interesting enough, but you can temper their impact by introducing contrasting elements. Tiles, for instance, can look cold and sterile, but with soft, fluffy towels or warm wood fittings you can redress the balance. Alternatively, you may exaggerate their qualities for dramatic impact by adding more hard, shiny details such as glass, mirrors or reflective metal. Many schemes play on a bold and simple interchange of pattern and texture. For example, contemporary themes often include pale, silky-smooth walls and crunchy coir matting to provide a low-key backdrop for sleek, pale wood furniture, dark iron accessories and vibrantly colored upholstery and accessories.

▲ *Matte and shiny surfaces, cool colors and warm wood tones create visual interest in this clean-lined contemporary-style kitchen.*

◀ *Warming shades of terra-cotta, together with a well-balanced contrast of large and small-scale patterns and rough and smooth textures, give this living room a lively glow.*

Pattern and Texture Checklist

Use this checklist to identify the balance of patterns and textures in your home. If the majority of items in a room fall under only one of the headings, the effect may be either bland or overpowering. If so, try introducing elements from one of the other lists to improve the balance.

PATTERN Dominant/Unobtrusive	TEXTURE Rough/Crunchy/Matte	Smooth/Shiny
Large/small scale	plaster	gloss paint
self-colored	wicker	chrome
mini print	damask	brass
stripes	slub cotton/silk	glass
checks	hessian/linen	mirrors
abstract	toweling	laminates
floral	sisal flooring	ceramic tiles
stylized motifs	untreated wood	marble
traditional	stone	polished wood/leather
contemporary	unglazed terra-cotta	glazed cotton/chintz

▲ *Smooth surfaces, fluid forms and cool, tranquil colors give this modern scheme its timeless elegance. Pattern detailing is minimal, but has dramatic visual impact.*

▲ *A cheery fabric print and patterned china work hard to complement the functional quality of the kitchen units and smooth, practical surfaces. Matte yellow walls and rustic accessories also soften the effect, to create a comfortable 'lived-in' look.*

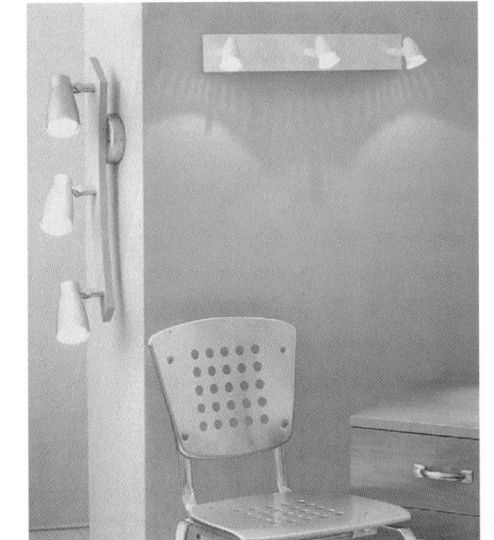

▶ *Shiny, matte, hard and soft are the qualities combined here in a subtle balancing act. Pattern also plays a part in creating this minimalist look, through the punched metal pattern and the rounded shapes of the lamps.*

WORKING WITH PATTERN

However bold they may be, patterns should maintain a balancing act in a room. They may appear on walls, floors, soft furnishings and accessories, or occur in a low-key way – a tracery of plant leaves, panel and cornice moldings or patterned tile details, for example. Furnishing fabrics are usually the most distinctive patterned elements in a room: with a printed or woven design, their textures can range from lightweight, lacy nets and glossy chintzes through subtle-shaded damasks to nubby exotic weaves and heavy velvets. You may choose a coordinated range of patterns as a way to introduce different scale designs into a scheme, and use them in toning colors for walls, furnishings and accessories.

It is the interplay of pattern qualities – using different scale and weight patterns and textures together – that brings a scheme to life. Tried and tested ready-made combinations often include a large floral with a mini-print chintz or wallcovering, as well as toning or contrasting plains. Other examples may be a boldy drawn fabric or an exotic, patterned carpet or rug with a restrained stripe or check.

▶ *Bold blocks of color and pattern for furnishings and accessories create a strong, sumptuous image which is tempered by the smooth, wooden floor and occasional furniture.*

◀ *This is a room of intriguing contrasts, where sinuously sensual forms and textures are dramatically set against a cool and neutral backdrop.*

▼ *Finding a good balance between pattern and texture is the key to creating interesting, individual decorating schemes.*

WORKING WITH TEXTURE

A room may look dull because the texture balance is poor, but often a few contrasting textures are all that is needed to bring a scheme to life. Light and shade create subtle changes on all textured surfaces. Texture also affects color: it can soften – think of velvet, matte paint, antique finishes, color-washed walls; it can reflect – smooth, shiny metal, high-gloss paint and ceramic tiles. Rugged, obvious textures, such as rough-cast plaster, exposed brickwork, distressed wood, wicker or coir matting work particularly well when they are contrasted with more subtle textures, such as smooth steel, glazed cotton and linen. It is this element of surprise that creates visual interest.

▲ *A rustic hearth becomes a dramatic focal point as the rich texture of the brickwork is enhanced with imaginative lighting and a few well-chosen accessories.*

▼ *The woven wicker furniture provides vital textural interest in this delicately color-coordinated bedroom. The lines of the painted wicker weave also link in a subtle way with the stripes of the bedcover. A matching floral print and formal picture arrangement add extra pattern detail.*

▲ *The fragmented pattern of the softly colored mosaic tiling and the muted, rather than high-gloss, sheen of metal accessories dispels any hint of a clinical look in this contemporary bathroom.*

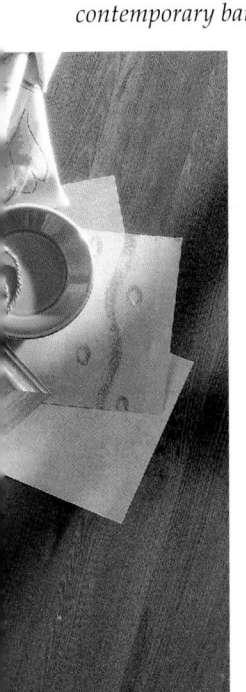

FINISHING TOUCHES

You can rebalance a jaded color scheme, or simply give a room a seasonal lift with pattern and texture details. A rug placed under a coffee table, brightly colored cushions on chairs and sofas, a well-placed mirror or a new group of pictures in coordinating frames all provide opportunies to introduce new life to a scheme. Plants and flower arrangements can also make a marked difference to a scheme. Arranged in rustic wicker baskets, sparkling glass or shiny ceramic containers to suit their style, they immediately create an impact.

> *Stylized stars, color-matched lamps, a classically framed print and dark, polished wood provide a formal pattern structure for a play on dark and light, matte and shiny. The warm-toned flower arrangement adds vitality, color and movement.*

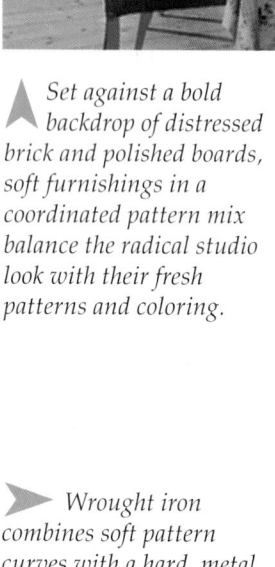

Here, the color balance is obvious and well considered, but the crunchy curtain tieback is an inspired visual link with the coarse basket weave.

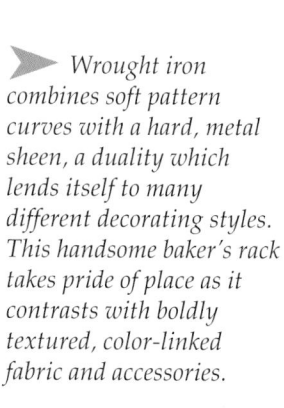

Set against a bold backdrop of distressed brick and polished boards, soft furnishings in a coordinated pattern mix balance the radical studio look with their fresh patterns and coloring.

> *Wrought iron combines soft pattern curves with a hard, metal sheen, a duality which lends itself to many different decorating styles. This handsome baker's rack takes pride of place as it contrasts with boldly textured, color-linked fabric and accessories.*

PATTERN AND SCALE

Consider the design and size of any pattern you use as a powerful tool to work visual tricks around your home, emphasizing or minimizing a feature or subtly setting the scene for the background.

◄ *Bold colors used in a well-balanced selection of patterns gives a pleasing harmony to this carefully planned scheme. A subtle stripe maximizes height and is further emphasized by a deep floral border; windows are accented with a medium-size, lively check. A large floral stripe focuses attention firmly on a welcoming sofa.*

Whenever you apply a pattern to a surface, whether it's a wall or a piece of furniture, the arrangement of lines and shapes in the pattern directly affects the way your eyes perceive the shape beneath. For example, a vertically striped pattern will have an elongating effect, making a wall appear higher than it really is. A pattern of dense, curvy shapes, perhaps a wallcovering strewn with large roses, will seem to advance towards you, pulling the walls in for an intimate, cozy feel, while finely drawn, scattered sprays of flowers have a lighter effect, seeming to open up the space.

You can use these effects to make the best of your home, by understanding the way patterns work in relation to scale. You can draw attention to particular objects, play down others, set a mood to suit the use of the room, and even visually change the shape of a room, all with the use of pattern.

When planning a room, bear in mind the effect of every object and surface within it. Often simple changes can be very effective – for example, staining alternate floorboards in different shades emphasizes their linear pattern, effectively widening a room in the direction of the floorboards. A strong pattern on a piece of furniture, perhaps a bold check, gives it more importance, and draws attention away from other less desirable features in the room.

25

Adjusting Room Scale

When choosing a pattern on a fabric or wallcovering, make sure you see a large sample of it and stand well away to view it from a distance as well as close up. It helps to half close your eyes, looking away and then back again to get a clear idea of how the pattern works. In addition to the lines and shapes that make up the design, don't forget that the colors themselves, and also the tonal values within them, are still at work. So a pattern of stripes in rich deep reds, while creating a sense of height, will counteract this with a welcoming warmth; the same pattern in cool pale blues will seem to open up the room even further.

> ➤ *The appealing shapes created by the eaves of this old house are accentuated by the pattern of twisting ribbons and knots of flowers as they carry the eye up to the ceiling line. A border would emphasize the shape further still, but may also serve to make the ceiling too low.*

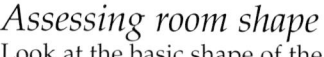

Assessing room shape

Look at the basic shape of the room you are working on, and decide what its advantages and disadvantages are. Most people are keen to maximize the height of their ceilings, to give a sense of space and air; but architectural conversions, where large rooms are divided up to create separate areas, often result in unwelcoming and awkward small rooms with disproportionately high ceilings. You may have a room with deeply sloping, asymmetrical eaves, or perhaps you have clumsily boxed-in pipes and cables you would like to hide.

▲ *A busy design of leaves on the walls and the contrast border conspire to conceal the fact that the ceiling of this room slopes sharply. The focus of the room is clearly the pretty arch, accented by the strong border which follows its curve.*

Pattern solutions

If a ceiling is too high or oddly shaped, take the wall pattern right across the ceiling to blend it in with the walls. Alternatively, adjust the proportions by breaking up the expanse of wall with a dado and picture rail. Concentrate attention below the dado with a large-scale pattern, balanced with a smaller, less dense design above. Bring the ceiling color down to the picture rail to blur the distinction between ceiling and wall.

If a narrow hall is a problem, black and white vinyl tiles set alternately in a diagonal pattern on the floor create an impression of width. You can easily copy the idea in wood or carpet for a similar effect.

To 'push out' the walls of a small room, choose a pattern with an obvious horizontal repeat or diagonal lines. Separate sprigs, splashy effects and wide shadow stripes all open up a space and make the most of a small room.

Stairwells are often awkward spaces, full of odd angles, and need a sense of proportion to feel welcoming. Here, a warm beige and honey scheme offsets the height, while a large trellis-based design above the dado makes the most of the space and adds breadth – echoed again in the carpet design.

Despite its cool turquoise scheme, this bathroom has been given a cozy, intimate air by extending the wallcovering over the ceiling, enclosing the room in a mist of golden stars.

The elegant proportions of a tall room are accentuated by vertical stripes. Decorative wallcovering borders balance the effect and draw attention to the lower half of the room.

If you are happy about the shape of your room, you may choose to emphasize it – you could paper a square, box-shaped room, for example, with a graphic windowpane check, or pick out a graceful arch with a scrolling stenciled border. Echo the shape of the arch around the room with an all-over scalloped design. If you find the interesting angles and unusual shapes of an older property appealing, make them more noticeable by taking a bold stripe up the walls, finishing in a matching border that follows the slope of the ceiling line faithfully.

27

SETTING THE SCENE

The general background that you create is very important, and influences the way you feel every time you walk into a room. A gently colored, regularly repeating but unobtrusive pattern used around the room can be more restful than a plain color, since it sets up a pleasing but noticeable rhythm that is satisfying to follow.

A well-chosen background pattern will effectively link together all the other elements of the room, playing down some elements and emphasizing others. A strongly patterned paper, for example, perhaps a richly colored ikat or a traditional damask, sets up such a strong rhythm around the room that your eye will skip over interruptions, such as an ugly pipe or a functional bookcase.

It's important to consider the blend of patterns around the room. They may be entirely different in design, ranging from florals and checks to exotic designs, but you should aim for a good balance of scale, from tiny motifs, through medium-sized designs to large, striking patterns. In general, use large patterns sparingly, mixed with a blend of the smaller and medium-scale designs.

◀ *This subtle ochre yellow background matches the other patterns in color and tone, but throws the vibrant check on the chairs and the vivid floral curtains into relief. A floral border links with the curtains and brings the room together.*

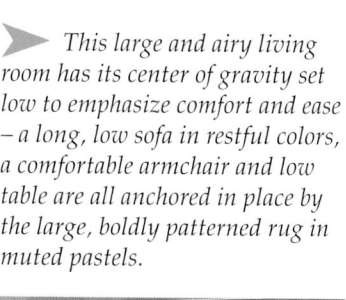

▶ *This large and airy living room has its center of gravity set low to emphasize comfort and ease – a long, low sofa in restful colors, a comfortable armchair and low table are all anchored in place by the large, boldly patterned rug in muted pastels.*

◀ *Envisage this room without the dramatic drape around the doorway, and it loses all its impact – the drape focuses attention on the doorway with its tempting balcony and view. The flowing lines of the pattern show well in the loose folds as they fall to the floor, and the colors cleverly link those of the blind and the surrounding wallcovering.*

In this bedroom, a vigorous pattern on the walls disguises the rather untidy-looking bookcase, which could otherwise dominate the room. Soft and pretty colors prevent the pattern from being too overpowering.

Visual highlights

You can use a bold pattern to highlight a particular feature, such as a special piece of furniture or a window treatment, in the same way as you would use color. A rich collection of coordinating patterned fabrics makes a wonderful splash of color at a window – a good place to use large, strong patterns since the window is a natural focus of interest in a room.

If a room lacks a focal point, use pattern to identify the heart of the room clearly. If you have a fireplace, highlight it in the traditional way by picking out the chimney breast in a different pattern, such as checks or stripes. Complement a sinuous chaise longue with the graceful scrolls of a traditional damask, or flatter the generous curves of a sofa with a flamboyant rose print. If you are unsure about large patterns, try them out on cushions to see how much zest and verve they can give a room.

In a bedroom, focus the pattern interest around the bed, coordinating a pretty drape, headboard and bedcover in restful but interesting patterns – florals are favorites, but there are many romantic prints with drifting clouds or cherubs to flavor your dreams.

This crisp and pretty bedroom illustrates the art of balancing pattern for a satisfying effect. Scattered floral sprays make a light, receding background, while a densely colored check picks out the distinctive headboards. Open windowpane checks and a small floral dress the bed, while a large rustic print at the window balances the headboards.

CHOOSING PATTERN SIZE

Handling patterns sometimes takes a little courage – many people are nervous about mixing patterns and even more nervous about using large-scale patterns. But a little confidence is well rewarded by a satisfying scheme, and there are many instances where a big, vigorous pattern injects life into an otherwise featureless room. A grand, opulent damask makes the most of tall windows, when a smaller design would look lost; large pieces of furniture, such as sofas, are equally able to hold their own, and actually look better treated in this way.

Alternatively, it's important to know when to scale the pattern down, offering interest without being out of proportion. This is often the case with a patterned wallcovering, where it links solid colors throughout the room, providing a background 'vibration' which is almost unconsciously picked up by your eyes to give an impression of continuity and harmony.

▲ An exuberant burst of cabbage roses covers the sofa in this simple and elegant room, ensuring its place center stage. The large pattern has nothing to compete with it – the plain background makes the perfect backdrop.

▲ The smart diamond pattern of this wallcovering sets a soft modern tone. Note how the tiny dots of coral red in the wallcovering add an unexpected spark, picking up the hot colors in the picture and jug.

▶ If you find large patterns intimidating, why not experiment with a couple of pillows? Here, bold contemporary florals are used for pillows to add zest to a cool blue and green scheme of checks and stripes.

TONAL BALANCE

*Successful decorating schemes depend on more than just a
pleasing choice of color and pattern; if, after a lot of careful planning
something still seems lacking, the tonal balance may need adjusting.*

When you achieve a good tonal balance in a scheme, using a blend of colors that creates a satisfying feeling of light and depth, the finished effect instinctively seems 'right'. Colors are affected not only by their intensity – how much pure color is in their makeup – but also by their tonal value. Tone refers to the lightness or darkness of a color, and how much white or black is present in its makeup. For an ideal tonal balance, the various tones in a scheme need to support and complement one another.

Even very different colors can share the same tonal value, so if too many colors of the same value are used together in a room, the effect will be disappointing despite the colorful potential. Too many pale tones result in a washed-out effect; too many mid tones look bland or dull, while an excess of deep tones looks gloomy and unsettling.

Whether starting from scratch on a scheme or trying to resolve an existing color problem, once you see how tonal balance works you can spot the tonal traps and effectively redress any imbalance. As a result, your decorating schemes will benefit from a more lively interest and tonal harmony.

▼ *These vibrant colors are perfectly at
ease together because they have a
good tonal balance. The expanse of light,
glowing yellow balances well with the
smaller area of cool, darker pink.*

CREATING TONAL BALANCE

Choices for color schemes are usually influenced by the quality of natural light in a room – daylight, as well as electric light, can dramatically affect tonal balance. On a sunny day, even the blandest of color schemes will take on a lively aspect, as pools of light create highlights and shadow patterns. You can use these natural highlights and shadows to show you where to use light, mid and deep color tones in a room.

Ideally, a range of tones should progress evenly through a scheme, without any dramatic jumps from one tone to another. Even in a totally black and white scheme, to be successful some broken color, pattern or light source should create subtle mid tones. From a practical viewpoint, it is often sensible to use mid tones for flooring, with lighter tones for walls. Darker tones for furniture and accessories will help 'ground' the scheme and create focal points.

Testing for tone

When you look at a black and white photograph of a room it becomes much easier to see the different tonal values of the colors. You can clearly see which tones are lighter or darker, and how they are distributed within the scheme. Without a camera to help, try half-closing your eyes to look at a room; if the colors seem to blend they probably share the same tonal balance. If you have access to a photocopier you can make black and white copies to check on the tonal balance of wallpapers, fabrics and paint swatches when planning a scheme.

▶ *Soft white and warm, earthy colors complemented by rich green accents provide a simple formula for a low-key yet visually stimulating color scheme. The cushion fabrics are an inspired touch as they mirror the dramatic flame colors, helping to pull the look together. The black and white print (below) shows how well the light, mid and darker tones of the scheme blend and balance, creating an inviting overall effect.*

▲ *Use paint charts as a reference for tonal values. Aim to balance light, mid and dark tones.*

Using paint charts

The simplest way to achieve good tonal balance is through a monochrome scheme, using varying tones of one color as a decorating theme. Paint manufacturers' color sample strips offer a quick reference for this type of tonal scheming; on each strip the colors are coded according to the proportions of pure pigment and their tonal value. A very successful approach when choosing a scheme is to select from the various levels of one strip to create a one-color scheme, and team this with neutrals or white, with perhaps a few different color accents.

You can also compare codings between different color strips for a scheme based on a variety of colors. If the codes tally, the colors share the same tonal values. Knowing this can be useful if you want to create a harmonious or contrasting scheme, and want to team matching tones or avoid using too many of the same value.

▼ Even a serene color scheme based on different shades of white or cream needs a little tonal excitement to elevate it from the mundane. Here, light wood furniture contributes mid-tone interest, while deeper wood tones and darker color accents complete the tonal balancing act.

An enveloping sense of light and space is created with minimal styling, white and soft mid tones and color splashes in stronger tones. The gentle shadows on the pale-toned sofa and curtains link these elements to the mid-tone floor, while the fresh color detailing ensures a vibrant effect.

The impact of natural light and shadow is used to dramatic effect on one shade of blue, creating a tonal change that adds to a harmonious sense of gentle color flow. Cool neutrals provide lighter tones, and warm violet blue accents balance the effect with their soft but deeper tones.

COLOR AND TONE

Just as a monochrome color scheme relies on a variety of tones to add intensity and bring it to life, so a mixed color scheme needs a selection of different tones from each color to give it vitality. The success of a color scheme is usually attributed to the colors used and the style of the decorations, but if the tones of the colors are too similar, the effect will be flat, even in a scheme based on potentially bold, bright colors. The solution is to include a range of light, mid and dark tones from each of the colors used.

Every room has good and bad points, which you can accentuate or disguise with different color tones. Permanent details such as skirting boards, door frames, moldings and cornices all help define the shape of a room, so deep or light color tones here will have quite an influence on the overall look of a scheme. You can define a handsome, dark fireplace against a light wall; or flatter a beautiful mid-tone timber floor with pale furnishings. Less favored items are improved by painting or covering them to blend with the background, so they 'fade' into the scheme. This also helps to create a spacious, uncluttered feel.

In this scheme based on contrasting yellow and blue, warm mid tones create a flattering background for lighter-toned features and darker, fine-lined accents. The classic white fireplace is a focal point, and this is balanced, and so enhanced, by the white chair and other light-tone touches – skirting boards and lamp shade – that help carry the eye around the room.

The deep wood tones and strong lines of this impressive fireplace are shown to advantage against a pale background. The proportions and dark tones of the carefully chosen period accessories achieve a perfect balance here, while the gleaming brass and contrasting white highlights add lighter visual elements.

PATTERN AND TONE

In a decorating scheme, patterns can create a vital color and tonal link with other features, effectively bridging and balancing areas of quite different tonal value. A print with a light background and a number of deeper-toned colors in its pattern can appear as an overall mid tone when seen in a large expanse against other tonal areas, as can a light pattern on a darker ground. This changeable quality gives you the opportunity to link colors from the scheme, at the same time maintaining a good tonal balance.

Patterns do not have to be used in any great quantity to have a noticeable tonal impact. Small splashes of pattern – even self-color patterns, used for accessories – can create tonal interest in a scheme. They lead the eye through the scheme, providing color and tonal highlights and accents.

Patterned fabrics provide many good examples of different tones working well together. Often several colors in a design will be a tonal match, with darker and lighter tones used for accents and backgrounds.

In this gentle aqua scheme, the colors in the framed prints and the patterns on the curtains create a harmonious link, both through color and tone. Their light backgrounds balance and offset the mid tones of the walls and table. Dark tones add tonal interest.

Similar mid-tone contrasts red and green could lose their impact, but the touches of vigorous acid yellow throughout the scheme provide reviving lighter tones. These are cleverly integrated into a happy mix of red and green checks and stripes.

Colors in similar tones can look more interesting when they appear together in a mix of different scale patterns and contrasting tones. These patterned accessories rely on white and a deeper toning plan for their satisfying tonal balance.

CREATING A MOOD

When you want to create a special mood in a room – to suggest an atmosphere that expresses a sense of place as well as your personality – make color and pattern your inspiration.

Decorating a room inevitably means you need to make choices – questions of room function, decorative style, lighting, colors, existing furnishings and cost are all key issues. With so many considerations, it helps to define the mood you would like to create before you make a start on the scheme.

Finding a direction is easier if you analyze your instinctive color and style preferences. Colors have certain characteristics which affect the way you perceive things. Everyone has favorites – a color can make you feel or look good, energize or relax you;

you can use color to make a room as warm and inviting as a sunny day, as blissful as a moonlit vista, or as fresh and airy as a cooling sea breeze.

Room size – whether it is large or small, dark or light – is largely irrelevant to creating a mood. While certain room styles tend to suggest a mood – soft modern and easy-going, dramatic and flamboyant or classic and restrained – it is color that really influences the 'feel' of a scheme. On the following pages you can see how compiling a collection of inspirational details can help you focus your ideas. Teamed with samples for

possible paint and fabric choices and ideas for accessories, you will have the makings of an evocative color scheme.

▼ Whatever your preferences may be for a particular decorative style, a room bathed in soft glowing pinks and burnt orange is going to be welcoming. Colors from the warm side of the color wheel have a comforting effect – a quality you can exploit in any size room.

DEFINING A MOOD

Inspirations for a scheme can come from many different sources. Your location may be a trigger for a certain mood, prompting you to long for an escapist theme, or you may wish to enhance your setting, bringing the shapes and colors from outside into your home. If you live in a town you may dream of the clear light and colors of the countryside, and decide on a color scheme and decorating style to remind you of this. If you relish the energy of your urban environment, you could celebrate this with a vibrant scheme based on hard-edge shapes, high-tech styling and the city colors of brick, stone and metal – highlighted by strong color splashes.

One of nature's serene sunsets inspires the balance of light and dark tones in this inviting scheme. Based on contrasts pink and green – also the colors of garden flowers – the effect is warm and homey, a mood that is enhanced by the simple cottage-style details.

Creating a mood board

Whatever your tastes, help to define your ideas for a mood with a collection – a scrapbook or collage – of things you like. Collect pictures from brochures and magazines of typical 'wish-I-were-there' shots of landscapes – windswept moors, lush tropical locations or exotic architecture, for example; follow where your mood takes you. Look at close-up colors and textures of fabulous food and fashion photography, reproductions of famous paintings and craftwork detailing. Gather clippings of anything that attracts your eye with its color and pattern, together with natural objects such as wood, pebbles or textiles, that capture the mood.

Arrange your findings on a corkboard or large sheet of cardboard, and prop them up in the room to be decorated. Look at your mood board in different lights to see how colors and patterns relate to one another. Rearrange, remove or add elements as desired until you have a color balance that you like.

> *Violet blue and orange may seem a bold choice for a color scheme, but seeing how successfully nature balances these elemental hues can be sufficient inspiration to get you started on a new look – one that expresses a more adventurous side of your personality. Based loosely on a dramatic evening sky, the mood here is vibrant and upbeat. Other influences to spur you on and complement your theme can come from details in magazines, such as these jewel-bright accessories.*

COLOR AND MOOD

The impact of color on a mood or atmosphere can never be underestimated. Follow your instincts for a color choice, then make use of the inherent characteristics of color – remember that warm colors advance, to make a room seem smaller, and cool colors recede, creating a more spacious feel. Whether you use colors full strength, muted or reduced to pale pastels, their qualities are still apparent.

PALE COLORS such as soft dove gray, light blue, lavender, aqua and mint green are well known for their soothing effects. This is why they have been a traditional choice for bedrooms, and in rooms where a sense of calm is desirable. White and pale neutrals often appear to fill a room with light – they can be warm or cool, and at their best create a spacious, elevating or romantic atmosphere.

STRONG COLORS are intense and demanding, with exaggerated qualities, depending on their position on the warm or cool side of the color wheel. Well known for dramatically altering the proportions of a room, use them to draw in the walls to create an intimate atmosphere, or to create bold focal points.

▲ Rich ochre walls seem to resonate with the heat and bright light outside. In this Mediterranean setting you can feel how much the room is at one with its surroundings.

◄ In a get-away-from-it-all mood, blue inspires quiet contemplation. Linked with warm, contrasting yellow, this room also reflects an individualist's touch.

► Calm, airy, elegant and restrained – or simply dull cream? For some, pale neutrals are inspiring, while for others they hold no interest – such is the power of color.

Early morning sunshine streams into this kitchen every day – or at least, that is what the atmosphere implies. Bursts of fresh green and yellow demonstrate their uplifting qualities.

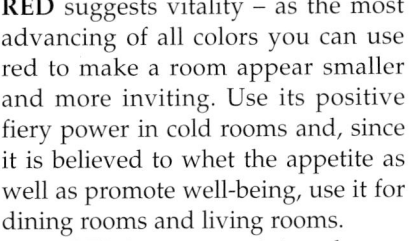

RED suggests vitality – as the most advancing of all colors you can use red to make a room appear smaller and more inviting. Use its positive fiery power in cold rooms and, since it is believed to whet the appetite as well as promote well-being, use it for dining rooms and living rooms.

YELLOW is an energizing, happy color, as expected from a color associated with the sun. Harness its get-up-and-go element by using it to lighten a dark room, to inject a little *joie de vivre* into a dull corner, or simply to enhance a sunny kitchen or dining room. Yellow is also the color of the intellect – teamed with neutrals you can make it the base for elegant and sophisticated schemes.

ORANGE shares many of the attributes of red and yellow. Use it for its welcoming qualities, and to contrast cool colors, grays, and neutrals.

GREEN is the living color, the color of nature. Positioned midway between warm and cool colors on the color wheel, it has a refreshing, balancing influence on a room. In its paler versions, green creates an optimistic, springlike atmosphere. All greens are complemented and enhanced by touches of warm color.

BLUE is linked with peace and harmony. Associated with the sky and sea, use its paler forms for spacious, calming effects. Warm up bolder shades of blue with contrast color accents and use strong blues to calm a brightly lit room.

PURPLE is the color of drama and nobility. It is also a mysterious color with a spiritual quality. Purple may have a warm or cool cast and, at its lightest, as heather, lavender and pale violet, looks restful and ethereal. Deeper purples need care – as plum and Imperial purple they are vibrant and intense, so temper these with pale neutrals to show them at their most dramatic.

41

MOOD AND STYLE

When you merge the character and personality of certain colors with a well-defined room style, you have the potential to create a scheme that says just what you want. In the close-up details of two rooms shown here, similar tints and shades of purple create quite different atmospheres.

Soft and gentle, this updated classic look suggests the influence of the great outdoors – you can almost imagine a fine mist lying over heather-covered moors. This effect is further emphasized by the muted tartans, rich textures and different tones used to build up the evocative atmosphere.

The styling is sleek and modern, but the difference in mood from the scheme above is striking. In this streamlined setting the purple tints and shades appear as controlled bursts of clear, jewel-bright color. The amethyst intensity is dramatically enhanced by the contrasting white walls and the fine lines of the glass and metal furniture and accessories.

The power of color is immense. It can enliven or subdue. It can grab your attention or melt into the background. It can make an object appear closer or farther away. The possibilities of color schemes are endless. The following pages present some of the most common choices for home decorating, and photographs show you how to work with them.

Monochromatic schemes offer much more variety than you might expect. Those of the primary colors, red, yellow and blue, show how intensity and pattern work to make these color schemes successful. Soft pastel and neutral schemes are naturally restful, but dramatic variations are a striking possibility. Black and white schemes are bold, yet they are used successfully in a variety of decorating styles. The historic colors of England and the United States utilize a wider palette that is generally muted, but they may be unexpectedly clear and bright. The harmonious spice colors are often warm and intense, but their cool and muted versions are also delightful.

YELLOW SCHEMES

Every tint and shade of yellow, from palest cream to deepest, glowing gold
has an energizing influence in a color scheme. It can bathe a cool room
with sunshine or create vital accents in a dark scheme.

When you choose yellow for a color scheme you introduce light and brightness to a room. In their many guises, yellow tints range from the barely-there yellows of buttermilk and pale primrose, through zingy citrus and radiant sunshine yellows to deep amber and golden ochre shades.

Traditionally, yellow is associated with energy and vitality; the sun, and daylight; warmth. As an active color it has tremendous impact in a decorating scheme. Busy areas such as a hallway, kitchen or dining room can all benefit from the invigorating influence of vibrant yellow. For a more relaxed atmosphere, there are the quieter yellow tones. Team them with soft harmonies and subtle contrasts for elegant, light-enhancing schemes. Yellow is a very versatile color; it needs careful handling not to overpower, but you can use it in its many variations throughout the home to raise your spirits and create a feeling of airy spaciousness.

Pale yellows

The palest yellows can provide a subtle alternative to white and play a neutral role in a scheme, creating a pale background for stronger color accents and gently harmonizing or contrasting schemes.

Pale yellows tinted with white and the merest hint of red create the warm, creamy buttermilk tints. Use these to brighten and add warmth to a cool room. Besides working well with stronger yellow tones, they liven up classic black or dark gray; pale, cool blues and greens; and stronger warm shades such as terra-cotta, blue and eggplant.

Cool pale yellows contain blue/green; think of orchids and green-tinged Christmas roses. As in nature, these tints balance and blend beautifully with pale warm pastels such as pink and apricot, and with deeper, leafy greens. They have a particularly restful effect in warm, sunny rooms.

◄ Warm cream schemes have a quiet calm; this atmosphere is enhanced by the elegance and simplicity of the styling details: a few graceful lilies, hints of gilt and mellow wood tones all play a softly harmonizing role.

◄ Cool pale yellow and soft gray are a classic combination. Here the basic scheme is lifted with touches of natural white and brighter yellow, and weighted by cooler, pale gold and green.

Citrus yellows

Citrus yellows are cool, bright and sharp and tinged with blue/green. They breathe spring into a scheme and have an acid edge. As a basically cool, bright tint, citrus yellows work well in clear light and in a naturally warm setting – as a background color in a sunny room or as a color splash against pure white in a kitchen. They can also create a mellow, Mediterranean look when used with gentle harmonies – pale lime green or warmer, muted orange and contrast blue.

At its most vibrant, citrus yellow's impact is dramatic. Teamed with white and strong brights and contrasts such as green and purple, or used to temper the strong neutrals gray and black, as well as shiny chrome and satin steel, its style is bold and elegantly contemporary.

A colorwash of bright citrus yellow and green creates a striking backdrop for neutrals, harmonizing greens and contrast blues. The effect is vibrant yet the simplicity of the scheme gives it a restful feel.

Pale lemon yellow walls create a cheerful background for a cozily cluttered sitting room. A bright citrus sofa cleverly balances the scheme.

Sunshine Yellows

As the name implies, sunshine yellows are the warm yellows containing varying amounts of red; sunflowers and buttercups sum up their strength. These most vibrant of yellows saturate a room with color when used extensively, 'shrinking' the walls to create an intimate atmosphere. This warming effect can work well in a cold light teamed with earthy reds and ochres, but in warmer situations can overpower unless it is handled carefully.

Such an energetic yellow requires restraint if it is not to swamp everything else, and often works best in small measures. Offset sunshine yellow against white or a pale neutral and an expanse of another strong color such as cool green or blue, or use it as a color accent for fabrics and accessories.

The play of dark and light is a fascinating theme. Here, the strong lines of dark metal furniture and accessories are dramatically silhouetted against sunny yellow walls.

Waking up to sunshine yellow on a dull day must promote the feel-good factor, but too much would be overpowering. Generous splashes of soft white and touches of deeper gold balance its impact.

◄ *Warm tints and tones of golden yellow are shown to advantage here with tiles and accessories in earthy pigment colors, set off with neutral brown and white.*

Deep Golden Yellows

The deep, mellow shades of golden yellow are shaded with black and may carry a touch of warming red or cooling green. They range through the shades of autumn leaves, curry and mustard spices, as well as the pigment colors ochre and old gold.

All variations of deep golden yellow have a muted glow, well suited to color schemes based on deeper, subtle harmonies and contrasts. They work wonderfully well in traditional schemes with period furnishings, linked with warm earthy colors such as rich terracotta, rose pink, lime, crimson and dark green. They also enhance Exotic-inspired schemes focused on neutral, natural looks, when complemented by dark brown and flashes of brilliant jewel color.

► *Mellow gold has a timeless elegance, displayed here through glints of gold and the warm, honeyed tones of the Classic furnishings and furniture.*

Yellow Accents

Just as a vase of brilliant yellow daffodils can lighten a room, or a bowl of zesty lemons create a lively table centerpiece, discreet touches or bold splashes of yellow can really liven up a scheme. Balance yellow accents throughout a room – and to the room beyond – so that the eye is held and carried through the scheme.

Yellow color accents need not be bold, although many schemes can benefit from its vital presence. You can introduce subtle yellow in a low-key way as a creamy or pale primrose alternative to white paint, and match the tint for lamp shades, vases or a fabric print. Work citrus yellow into a quiet blue or green scheme through tassel and braid trims on cushions and lamp shades, the piping on furniture covers or as details in a floral print. Stronger yellow accents work well as short sharp statements on wall cupboards, chair covers, a dramatic window blind or a glossy painted door – and simply as an exuberant display of glowing sunflowers.

Citrus yellow, green and white are colors made for one another. As a group, these pillows would brighten a plain sofa or add a splash to neutral wood or wicker garden seats.

The perennial appeal of sunflowers needs no explanation: with their cheerful simplicity and vibrant looks they bring summer into any room.

Chinese yellow is a classic, well-loved color; its bright acid tones lend a freshness to pale schemes as well as to bright contrasts – as demonstrated by the colorful motifs on these plant pots.

Buttercup yellow paintwork brings out the glowing colors in this well-loved William Morris print, giving the traditional scheme an energetic modern twist.

RED SCHEMES

*When you choose red for a color scheme you make a commitment to
verve and vitality. In all its variations – from hot scarlet to deep,
glowing crimson and burgundy – red is rich, warm and welcoming.*

As an emotive color, red symbolizes many powerful feelings: strength, passion, heat, anger – and danger. It is traditionally linked with grand occasions and opulent period style, and at its richest and deepest, red can look sumptuous, exotic or overtly theatrical.

Red is essentially a warming, 'advancing' color – a color that seems to come toward you. It has the effect of 'drawing in' a space, so you can use it to make a room more intimate and cosy. Red also makes objects appear larger – a useful ploy for creating a focal point with furniture or soft furnishings. You can also use red for details and accessories to create a visual spark in a room.

Reds are naturally enhanced by all types of green as they sit opposite each other on the color wheel. Versatile reds can have the warm, yellow cast of scarlet and pimiento, or the cooler, blue quality of crimson and the wine reds. You can tint reds with white until they are rose pink or coral; temper them with deeper harmonies – the plums, russets and purple shades – or team them with pale neutrals and black. They also look wonderful with orange, ochre and yellow in hot and spicy schemes.

You can tame the intensity of red through pattern – red and white checks, stripes, florals, tartans and toile de Jouy – and with broken color glazes and paint effects.

As a general guide to working with red, remember a little goes a long way. Aim to balance its effect, so the eye can link different touches throughout the room. Always check color matches; two distinct reds may not work well together. Try a red sample against other colors – that warm red may have a surprisingly cool tone, or the other colors may appear different. Reds may spell danger, but they can be well worth the risk.

Vermilion and scarlet

Together with primary red these are the hottest and most brilliant reds: the reds of poppies, tomatoes, holly berries and true-love hearts. They team harmoniously with yellow and orange, as well as with deeper blue-reds and bright, hot pinks. These reds often sizzle in exotic silks and Madras cotton checks, and look bright but less intense, teamed with white as gingham checks and folk-art inspired patterns.

As the most powerful of the reds, balance these carefully to avoid an overwhelming effect. On walls they create instant atmosphere, and look smart teamed with muted, cooler colors: soft browns, grays, old golds and ochres. As color splashes, hot reds look particularly good in kitchens and children's rooms – for window blinds, accessories and linen.

▲ As close neighbors on the color wheel, hot red and orange are always at ease with each other, as their fiery natures are balanced together. Here, warm, neutral wicker and wood tones, and flashes of white and cream provide a subtle breathing space among the glowing harmonies.

◄ Bathed with light, bright broken reds teamed with mellow honey tones create a warm and welcoming effect despite the large proportions of the room. A play of red stripes, checks, prints and solids helps to boost the comfortable effect.

Hot and muted, this dusty red has a sun-baked quality reminiscent of the earthy reds of the Mediterranean or American Southwest. It is a red that is complemented by touches of deep, bright green and simple, rustic styling.

Muted and rusty reds

These reds can appear warm or cool depending on their makeup. They have a brick red, earthy quality, seen in the pigment-dyed red yarns used in many eastern rugs and textiles. Muted reds are familiar as American Country-style Barn red, and as sun-baked Mediterranean and Mexican red. Chinese red – so perfectly balanced with traditional lacquered black – is a perfect example of a hot, rusty red.

Use these reds with other slightly muted shades – gray-green, indigo blue, ochre and beige – and with their opposites turquoise and jade green, for a low-key look. For a stronger effect, try them with warmer muted pinks and coral. Bright cactus green also works with the slightly parched look of these reds, and they are naturally sympathetic to the rich shades of warm cream.

With its rosy glow, this muted red has tantalizing hints of deep crimson and golden brown in its makeup. Used as a colorwash, and finished with a gold stenciled border, the effect is rich and mellow.

53

Crimson

Crimson reds are the majestic, jewel colors of garnets and rubies. Slightly cooled, and edging toward the blues on the color wheel, they are synonymous with sumptuous velvets and brocades, and glow against Classic-style dark wood furniture, gilt-framed pictures and sparkling crystal.

As a red with a depth that demands to be taken seriously, deep crimson is a traditional choice for walls in period-style dining rooms, sitting rooms, halls and Dramatic-style bedrooms. You can complement its theatrical overtones with deep forest green, as well as with lime, and by a liberal addition of gold and metallic accents.

Crimson red is often seen in tartans, and in traditional floral prints – where its impact is often enhanced by a pale ground scattered with strong blues, yellows and greens. It also appears tinted with white to a powerful rose pink in more delicate period-style designs such as toile de Jouy fabrics, as seen in the window shades on page 97.

> *Crimson's reputation as an aid to digestion has made it a traditional choice for elegant dining rooms. Crimson looks splendid by day or candlelight, and is a perfect foil for period-style furnishings.*

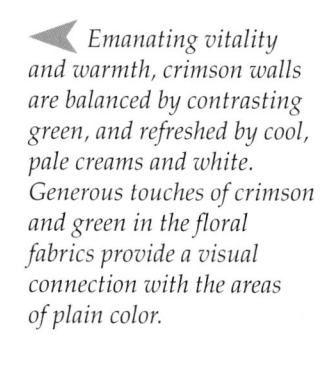

> *Emanating vitality and warmth, crimson walls are balanced by contrasting green, and refreshed by cool, pale creams and white. Generous touches of crimson and green in the floral fabrics provide a visual connection with the areas of plain color.*

Wine reds

Burgundy and claret reds are, as the names imply, strong and full-bodied. These heavy, cooled reds may have a hint of grape, plum or damson in their makeup, and perhaps a russet tinge. Their weight lends them distinction, and their depth makes them a more subtle choice as a base for a color scheme than the brighter crimson reds. Wine reds are naturally complemented by bronze green, deep olive, sage and cooled golds, as well as by rich russet, red-brown and by pale, yellow-tinged gray-green. These colors are often combined in rich, period-style textiles and fabric prints.

For a modern color scheme based on wine reds, you could balance their depth with deep marine blue, and by teaming them with a range of harmonies from the same red family, starting with raspberry pink, enlivened with small touches of olive or lime, and with warm-toned satin sheen metallic details. Paler wine reds would also look fresh against a citrus-tinged pastel white.

Formal and distinguished, the traditional place for deep wine red is as an elegant backdrop to Classic-style furnishings. Here, the neutral shades of the framed prints are thrown into relief by the rich plum red walls, which in turn enhance the warm-toned wood and echo the extravagant reds of the flower display. Gleaming silver provides the perfect foil for these sumptuous tones.

Classic fabric designs using reduced strength versions of a strong red offer an effective way to integrate areas of stronger toning color in a room, or simply an opportunity to enliven a cool neutral period-style scheme. These beautiful furnishings suggest gracious living on an opulent scale.

RED ACCENTS

You have only to look at a vase of scarlet roses or the plush, deep crimson tones of anemones or peonies to see how powerful reds can be. In their many subtle variations, reds can look wonderful set against glowing harmonies and wood tones, and inject cool neutrals with vital color accents.

That well-known expression 'less is more' applies to all varieties of red when you use it as an accent color – you really do need only a small amount for it to make an impact. Red details and accessories work best if they are echoed throughout a room – a group of scarlet silk or crimson print cushions, balanced by two pretty red candle shades; a hint of red in a picture, or in a fabric print – any red detail will draw the eye, so it helps to balance a large splash with smaller, or fragmented patches of red.

Red has such positive connotations that you can use it to highlight good points and, despite its high profile, effectively disguise lesser features. A smart red check fabric will accentuate the attractive curves of a comfortable armchair, just as a glossy primary red, by virtue of its sheer brilliance, will eclipse any flaws and instill new life into a tired chest of drawers or dresser.

▶ *With the addition of a geranium red slipcover, a simple chair looks contemporary and chic. In a cool neutral and metallic scheme, it demands attention, and is perfectly balanced by the matching red lamp shade. The toning pink picture frame and vivid blue glass add extra color notes.*

▲ *Venetian red crystalware has exactly the rich ruby tones to flatter polished dark wood and sumptuous furnishings. As a crimson red, it suggests festive cheer and a sense of good living.*

▶ *Earthy red and a strong but muted blue are a comforting base for a warm, Country-style scheme. As a bold accent, the red and white check chair cover balances the areas of strong color beautifully, and echoes the broken blue and white of the floral fabrics.*

BLUE SCHEMES

*Blues can be calming and tranquil, vibrant and demanding
or deep and mysterious – draw on their many moods and qualities
to create intriguing, atmospheric color schemes.*

Blue has a wonderfully evocative quality – as the color of the sea and sky it conjures up images of elemental vastness, and is traditionally seen as the balancing color of harmony and peace. It therefore lends itself to rooms where a quiet, calming atmosphere is desirable.

Primary blue is a cool color, situated on the color wheel midway between the warm primaries of red and yellow. Depending on its cast, it can take on the warmer influence of red – eventually turning to purple and magenta – or absorb the more subtle warming qualities of yellowed green, moving through deep marine blue to turquoise.

Most blues, whether light, dark or muted, are seen to advantage balanced with warmer contrasts – yellow and blue are a classic combination – and with warm-toned neutrals such as soft cream, camel and brown. Because blue is a cool color, it appears to recede, so you can use it to advantage to create an optical illusion of space, or to calm a sunny, brightly lit room.

The combination of blue and white – from pale to dark blue – has an unbeatable freshness, whether it is used as broken color through patterns and textures, or as vivid color accents. Whichever quality of blue you use, whether tinted with white to a pale pastel blue, or darkened to a deep royal blue, blues blend well together in a scheme. There are harmonies too – from the blue-reds or blue-greens – and contrasts such as yellow, lime, orange and red to flatter a blue scheme.

PALE BLUES

Pale blues are an excellent choice for creating a cool and airy atmosphere, one where a sense of space is maximized. Made by adding substantial amounts of white to the basic blue, their brilliance is reduced to a delicate, warm or cool blue tint. When you want to create a restful mood, pale pastel blues – either greeny-aqua blue or rosier, baby blue – team beautifully with white or pale cream to create a gentle, romantic look.

The greener tints of pale blue can evoke the blues of Scandinavian color schemes, lit by a clear but cold northern light. Balance these chilly blues with soft yellow, ochre, warm white and mellow, honeyed wood tones. Pale blues also work well with sugar almond pastels, either as a medley of colors against white, or in delicate patterns and plains.

Although they are soothing favorites for nurseries, bedrooms and bathrooms, pale blues also work well in busier settings. They look sparklingly fresh and clean in a kitchen – china collections are a traditional blue favorite – and with splashes of accent color such as red, yellow or green. In a warm sitting room, pale grayish blues look calm and elegant – try teaming them with delicate turquoise or duck-egg blue and pale cream and with silver or pewter metallic accents.

▶ *Soft milky white provides a subtle foil for pale, colorwashed blue paneling. The delicate coloring is enhanced by deeper blue and the little touches of mauve and yellow.*

◀ *Dramatically simple, with a look that owes much to the cool, fresh influence of Scandinavian style, gentle, green-toned aqua blues look serene in an all-white setting, offset by metallic glints, shiny glass and just the smallest touches of warming pink and yellow.*

MID-BLUES

Mid-blues are the hazy sky blues – those almost clear bright blues that are neither dark nor light, and balance so well with paler and darker blues. Pleasant to live with, especially when balanced with an expanse of flattering white or cream, warm-toned mid-blues have sufficient impact to make their presence felt without being overpowering. In their warmer tones, mid-blues can work well as a cosy background color for walls in almost any room – especially in a monochrome scheme with other tones of blue, and highlighted with palest yellow or white. In their cooler tones, mid-blues and grayed mid-blues need careful balancing to prevent them from looking bleak or dull. These blues respond to the warming influences of soft peach, coral pink, terra-cotta and cream – colors that help to maintain a good warm/cool balance.

Mid-blues look fresh and bright as accents in apple green and brilliant white schemes, or mellow in schemes based on the cooler spice colors and warm, vanilla white. Mid-blues hold their own in patterns, particularly in fresh, country-style florals and more formal period designs, and are almost a classic feature in checks and stripes.

▲ *Broad sky blue and white stripes work well as a background pattern, as they are balanced by a generous sweep of soft white used for the carpet and chair covers. Such strong pattern needs low-key support in this way, while the paler and deeper touches of blue – in the wall plates, checks and deep blue table, maintain a good tonal balance.*

▶ *A blue and white scheme offers a marvelous opportunity to juggle a variety of different scale patterns together, to create a lively visual balance. Here, the checks and floral design create a focal point against the calming blue and white of the background.*

> *In a sunny room, warm-toned china blue looks cozy and inviting. Fresh touches of white, and a play of blue and white patterns and textures – in the wall plates, bed linen and the bed frame – add up to a charming, romantic scheme.*

DEEP BLUES

Deep blues include strong cobalt blue, the rich blues of lapis lazuli, glass bottle blue, the Mediterranean sky – and sometimes the sea – and the traditional china blues, familiar as the vibrant willow pattern and Delft blue.

As blues deepen, more caution is needed when you use them prominently in a scheme. They can be intense and demanding, so are best used in smaller, measured amounts. As with all blues, they look magnificent with white, so you can risk using deep blue on the walls in a room where paler blues and white are a strong feature – as the main furnishing colors; or turn the plan around and use deep blue for the furnishings. You can soften their impact, while retaining their dramatic effect, by teaming deep blues with paler harmonies. For example, try green-toned deep blues with aqua green and turquoise, or warmer deep blues with mauve and lavender.

Deep blues make powerful accent colors; with white naturally, and with cool neutrals and paler blues. They strike a balance with paprika red, where they can take on a rustic look reminiscent of Scandinavian and German folk art designs; and with grayed, mustard and ochre yellows or red, they have a vibrantly Mediterranean, Provençal look. For a bright, contemporary look, try teaming deep blues with splashes of strong shocking pink or orange, or let them zing alongside lime and bright sunshine yellow.

▲ *Intense deep blue could be overpowering, but in this contemporary scheme it is calculated to create a dramatic impact, balanced with harmonizing aqua, and carefully balanced accents. Here, shocking pink, yellow and apple green add vital color highlights.*

MARINE BLUES

Familiar as navy blue and teal blue, these blues are the coolest of the blues, with a considerable amount of yellow, green and gray/black in their makeup. In their palest form they have a 'water's edge' quality, and as such, blend naturally with deeper marine tones. As with all the blues, blending several blues from the same family together in varying tones in a scheme seems to underline their subtle, often restful qualities.

A color scheme based on dark marine blue and white or cream, with perhaps a touch of gold, yellow or red as an accent color, has the same smart impact expected from a black and white scheme, but the overall look is softer. Marine blue and white stripes and checks make a sofa look tailored and elegant, or use marine blue pinstripes as a wallcovering, balanced with larger stripes or toning plain soft furnishings. Then introduce contrast accents for accessories. In a bathroom or child's bedroom, make marine blues the basis for a jaunty nautical or seaside theme, with white and little touches of red or yellow.

On a more subtle note, there are the muted, grayed marine blues such as American country Shaker blue. These respond well to contrasts in other muted shades, such as Barn red – a muted spicy red – and grayed greens and mustards.

Just like its namesake Shaker style, Shaker blue is a plain and simple color; cool and slightly muted, its straightforward appeal makes it ideal for functional pieces, and a perfect complement to reds and golden ochre.

A pattern of finely drawn stripes creates an atmospheric background for a formal arrangement of pictures and period furnishings. Further visual interest is created by the floral prints and unusual, broadly checked daybed cover.

BLUE ACCENTS

Neutral and natural schemes can be ideal settings for an injection of blue – perhaps as one beautiful accessory such as a chair or bedcover, a stunning lamp, in a framed print or vase of flowers. Its close links with nature allow little touches of blue to suggest a hint of summer sky or sparkling sea in a room, whether the style is a simple Country look, outrageously Dramatic, or a more traditional, Classic style.

Choose one isolated blue piece – as a focal point – or group several blue pieces together for balance and impact.

▶ *The delicate mid-blue checks in this pretty cream and white bedroom are complemented beautifully by the splash of balancing contrast yellow.*

◀ *In a contemporary scheme based on vibrant color brights, the color balance between a simple yellow flower in a deep blue glass makes a dramatic style statement.*

◀ *Warm-toned wood provides a beautifully mellow background for a soft blue colorwash. The creamy wall color may be cool and grayed, but it illustrates the enduring contrast theme of blue and yellow.*

▲ *An understated scheme based on clear whites, soft neutrals and naturals provides the perfect background for color accents. Here, a rich blue blanket gives depth to this simple scheme, as well as a definitive touch.*

PASTEL SCHEMES

Choose pale and chalky pastel colors for their calm and restful qualities, or take the new generation of stronger pastels to create vibrant, light-enhancing schemes.

Pastels have always been appreciated for their softness and for the unassuming way they blend into a scheme, often playing a supporting role for stronger colors.

True pastels are made by tinting pure white with color, to create a much reduced version of the original hue. In decorating terms, pastels can range from the palest tinted whites, through the familiar 'sugar almond' colors of baby pink, powder blue, lilac and pale pistachio green, and the innumerable soft tints of artists' pastels, to the stronger yet still chalky, 'sorbet' colors and new, sharp 'synthetic' pastels.

When pastels share the same tonal values you can mix them together freely in gentle harmonies and subtle contrasts, and work them from room to room for easy-on-the-eye continuity. The palest pastels combine well with stronger pastel accents as well as black, gray, naturals and metallic accents. Mixed to a more intense quality, pastels help create a bright, contemporary feel. Used full strength these colors could be startling, but diluted with white and tamed, pastels need never be dull.

Sugar almond pastels are soft and delicate, but they need never look insipid. Used generously with neutrals and as stronger pastel accents, their freshness complements many contemporary room schemes.

WORKING WITH PASTELS

Because pastel colors are so versatile they often play an important role in a scheme yet remain understated. With their gentle, light-enhancing characteristics, pastels span many different decorating styles from traditional Classic looks, through soft and muted Country styles to brighter, Contemporary schemes.

Used in a cool, north-facing room, warm-tinted whites and stronger tones can compensate with a warming glow, just as cool pastels can lighten and 'enlarge' a small or crowded room. For walls, pastels in flat emulsion, two-tone colorwashes and other broken color paint effects, such as sponging or ragging, are particularly effective. These can create a subtle feeling of depth and texture without being obtrusive, and the different tones can provide a subtle link with soft furnishings and other features.

Pale tints on furniture – limed and color-washed wood – are another pastel option. Blending the color of wood with a pastel scheme in this way helps create a light, airy feel and contributes to a pleasing color flow.

Pastel monochromes A simple way to create a spacious feel in a small room is with a pastel monochrome scheme – one based on deepening tints of one pastel color. On its own, or linked with white, black or neutrals, you can echo the tint throughout the scheme, so the finished effect strikes a good tonal balance of light, dark and mid tones.

Pastel harmonies Two or three pastel tints close to one another on the color wheel, such as pale gold, apricot and pink, provide a harmonious base for a warm scheme. Use pastel harmonies as expanses of plain color, or work them together as patterns and textures. To create restful color schemes, link pastel harmonies with accents in stronger versions of the same colors or with gentle contrasts, as well as with white or neutrals.

Pastel contrasts As gentle pastels, color wheel opposites such as pink and green, or subtle contrasts such as palest blue and yellow or soft lilac and lime become charming, highly usable versions of their original colors. Try using pastel contrasts in equal intensities, but with one dominant tint. Highlight the scheme with lashings of white, and perhaps one or two stronger versions of the tints for accents. Alternatively, work with a more extensive palette of mixed 'sugar almond' pastels, again teamed with white, or with an expanse of one of the pastel tints to balance.

> *Ice cream pastels pink and green create a carefully balanced total look. The pale, matching painted furniture plays a crucial role in blending the different elements together.*

◀ Cool, Scandinavian style influences this pastel scheme based on gentle contrasts, blue and yellow. The soft colors are shown to advantage by darker toning accessories and warm-toned neutrals.

▼ Facing doors offer a wonderful opportunity to create a color flow through several rooms. Here, harmonizing pastels of blue, lavender and mint contrast softly with pale rose pink.

STRONG PASTELS

Vibrant and clear, yet with an underlying chalkiness which tips them into the pastel category, the new, strong pastels have a young, contemporary look. They take inspiration from the 'synthetic' pastels derived from modern colors such as shocking pink and acid green, and the sun-bleached colors of the Mediterranean. These stronger tints demand attention wherever you use them, and so look their best playing a balancing act with one another.

One easy way to introduce strong pastels is as vivacious color accents, teamed with quieter pastels or white. A clean-lined sofa, upholstered in a lively pastel tint such as pale acid orange makes a simple, contemporary color statement against a soft white or palest baby blue background. Similarly, cushions in strong pastels work in the same way on white or neutral seat covers. As these pastels have such verve, they are a natural choice for fresh, summery schemes and outdoor living – and for creating chic, simple looks to suit any budget.

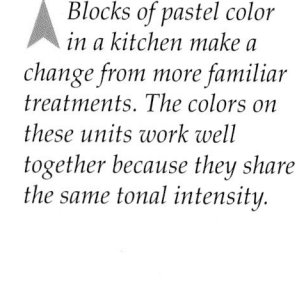

The success of this bedroom scheme owes much to the way the cool pastel mauve and vibrant pink are combined. Reliable white tempers what could be an overwhelming effect and, in the curtain fabric, provides a subtle tonal link between the two main colors.

Strong pastels suit Contemporary-style accessories very well; they share an exuberant spirit, but are rarely 'over the top'.

Blocks of pastel color in a kitchen make a change from more familiar treatments. The colors on these units work well together because they share the same tonal intensity.

In a low-key setting, one based on quiet neutrals, pale tints and clean-lined furnishings, the new generation of vibrant pastels creates a dynamic focal point.

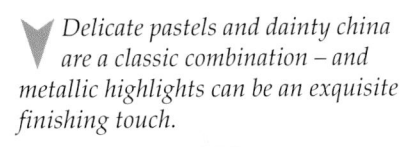

Delicate pastels and dainty china are a classic combination – and metallic highlights can be an exquisite finishing touch.

Set against an airy backdrop and clear bright white, a pastel pink sofa makes a simple color statement. Blue pillows and a splash of pastel green on the window blinds complement the stylish effect.

PASTEL PATTERNS

Delicate florals, dainty prints and pretty stripes and checks sum up many pastel patterns. These well-loved designs form the base for many traditional pastel schemes – soft looks for babies' nurseries, romantic bedrooms, bathrooms – and support calm, restful schemes anywhere in the home.

To steer this essentially pretty look away from becoming too 'sugary-sweet', it is important to use pastel patterns in well-balanced proportions. Team them with toning plains, either gentle harmonies or contrasts, or flatter the soft patterns with bolder accent colors. Take a look at the pastel colorways of ready-made coordinated accessories – where two or more different scale patterns may be teamed together – to see how these patterns balance. Use this format as a guide to linking different patterns such as florals with stripes or checks. As with stronger colored patterns, the simplicity or complexity of the finished effect is a matter of choice – pastel patterns may be softened, but they can still carry a punch that belies their pale and interesting origins.

➤ *Lavender blue walls create a restful atmosphere for relaxed dining. The coloring of the fabric print is actually a very strong pink and white, but blended together the two colors become a pastel shade, and balance well with the background.*

▼ *Coordinated furnishings in soft pastel yellows and greens bring an air of freshness to a bedroom. The wood tones of the floor and wardrobe are a welcome warming influence.*

▲ *Nostalgic Country style is given an update with strong pastels. Shocking pink tinted with white to pastel status, and teamed with cool, fresh white, creates a flattering backdrop for floral bed linen and accessories in lively pastel colors.*

NEUTRAL SCHEMES

*Calm and unpretentious, or strikingly bold
in their simplicity, the subtle tones of neutral schemes
bring an understated elegance to home styling.*

Choosing a neutral color scheme gives you plenty of options. Any scheme based on subtle, smudgy neutral tints and shades can, in typical chameleon style, take on whatever character you want it to. True neutral colors are black, white and gray. Gray is made from a blend of black and white with a little dash of color from anywhere on the color wheel, which makes it infinitely adaptable.

In decorating terms, soft brown – basically a mix of red, blue and yellow muted with black and white – and lighter honey tones, taupe, buff, beige, mushroom and cream are also known as neutrals. Like gray, these are tantalizing shades; they can be warm or cool, with an underlying tinge of color that appears to change in different lights, and when placed with colors.

This means that decorating with neutrals is not the easy option it may seem. Balancing whites, off-whites and a myriad of subtle shades in a scheme takes just as much care as working with stronger color. Once the balance is right however, you have a wonderful setting for a play of accents, textures and surfaces.

▲ *One of the pleasures of a neutral color scheme is discovering how different patterns and textures are enhanced by the delicate, understated neutral shades. In their quiet way neutrals create a harmonious, fluid balance quite unmatched by stronger color schemes. In this room every element is a delight to the eye as the shape and form of each accessory adds to the sum of the whole.*

Neutral Schemes

A neutral color scheme can provide a welcome oasis in the brash glare of busy modern living. An abundance of pale shades and soft tones is visually restful, and can create an airy, spacious atmosphere, even in a small room. They also enhance the shape of the room and lead the eye easily through an open-plan scheme, emphasizing its bold lines. A light, well-balanced neutral scheme also seems to eliminate clutter, by quietly reducing the visual impact of disparate features or bulky furniture.

The beauty of neutrals is their versatility; they suit many different decorating approaches, from Classic, elegant styles, through sophisticated Contemporary looks to rustic Country effects. Some people avoid using pale neutrals, assuming that they are impractical, yet many neutral paint finishes, fabrics and floorcoverings are easy-care, and the rewards of a light and airy scheme can outweigh any slight disadvantages. If necessary, you can always incorporate darker neutral colors – perhaps charcoal gray and brown, or warm wood shades for mottled or heavily textured upholstery or flooring – and use lighter neutrals elsewhere.

▲ *A good tonal balance and an interesting mix of patterns and textures ensures a neutral scheme will never look dull. Checks are a theme here, and this is echoed in a subtle way through the wicker headboard and squared picture mats.*

▼ *An intricate blend of patterns and textures in cream, warm beige and brown, complement the cool, soft neutral tones of marble and stone. Dramatic black and hints of earthy red and soft green provide understated accents.*

▲ *For a soft white or monochrome scheme, a little shimmer and sheen can provide flattering highlights in what could be an unremarkable color effect. Glazed fabric, gilt picture frames and shiny metal accents all add a change of pace.*

Neutral textures The most successful neutral schemes contain a satisfying blend of textures. In the absence of distracting color, these take on added importance; it is the visual play between various elements – rough with smooth; hard with soft; shiny with dull – and a balance of shade and tone that brings the scheme to life.

Contrast smooth marble, ceramic tiles and shiny wood with velvet or nubby weaves for upholstery, throws or rugs. Blend woven checks or raised rib stripes, smooth cotton, soft wool and coarse linen with cork or chunky fiber matting, distressed wood or wicker. Always take the opportunity to contrast different textures in a range of light, mid and darker neutral tones.

Glossy neutrals In a neutral scheme, reflective surfaces such as glass, polished wood and gleaming metal, or an expanse of shiny glazed chintz or satin, contribute new surface interest. These additions work particularly well in monochrome schemes based on one neutral color, and with soft harmonies, where they add zest to the finished effect. These glossy neutrals can be understated – walls with a soft sheen, for example, or a pale, satin-finish floor. Or you can use them as hard-working accents – gilt frames, candlesticks, brass or burnished metal curtain poles, lamp bases and tabletop accessories.

▲ *Familiar glossy bathroom features such as mirrors, glass, shiny paint and gleaming metal all create ready-made surface interest in a soft and neutral color scheme.*

71

NEUTRALS AND NATURALS

Neutrals and naturals blend very comfortably together, so much so that the combination is often a key feature in modern, low-key decorating schemes. The subtle textures and warm or cool tones of polished and distressed wood, sisal, rush or coir matting, and unbleached cottons and linens, are enhanced by pale, soft neutrals as well as by bolder brown, black and white. Use naturals to create a total look, or introduce them into a scheme for accessories, accents and small details.

Take inspiration from the complex blends in nature's neutrals. A handful of sand, for example, reveals shades that range from warm gold, through cool gray to palest cream. Rocks and pebbles have dappled patterns and intricate stripes based on monochrome effects and gentle contrasts – cool, yellowed beige and blue-gray, or greenish white and warm earthy brown – the variety is endless. With a little imagination you can translate these into schemes, as paint effects and through fabrics and prints.

Neutrals and naturals, straight lines and curves – a collection of polished wooden objects has a harmonious visual link with the surrounding wood surfaces.

The bold taupe and white patterned wallcovering creates a sympathetic background for the stronger wood tones. The warm coloring also helps to link the disparate styles of the furniture. Cooler fabrics and accessories in stone and soft white balance the restful neutral scheme.

WHITE SCHEMES

The impact of an all-white or mainly white scheme is dramatic. The sense of space and light can be quite dazzling, and white provides a wonderful backdrop for clean-lined modern furniture and natural materials. In its purest form white is a total absence of color, but most decorating whites have the merest touch of color, so they can 'read' as soft, 'natural' white or appear sharp and cool. Some paint manufacturers produce whites tinged with the palest of pastel tints, and these are designed as a starting point for stronger, color-linked and coordinated schemes.

Matching up different shades of white can be tricky, but if you aim for a basic 'warm' or 'cool' white scheme, and team this with stronger 'off-whites' and neutrals to harmonize or contrast, you can achieve a good balance.

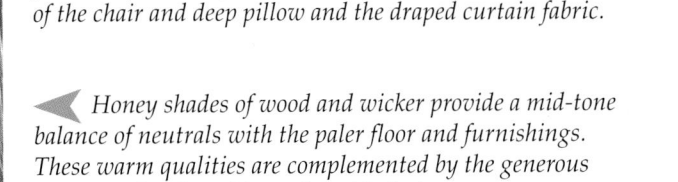

▲ *For graphic simplicity and dramatic effect, an all white scheme, highlighted with black and just the merest touch of warming stone beige, makes an elegant neutral combination. A penchant for luxury is indulged in the gracefully plump curves of the chair and deep pillow and the draped curtain fabric.*

◄ *Honey shades of wood and wicker provide a mid-tone balance of neutrals with the paler floor and furnishings. These warm qualities are complemented by the generous splashes of cooler white and the black elements.*

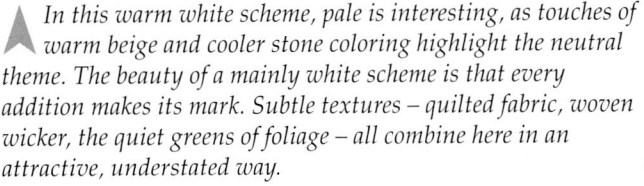

▲ *In this warm white scheme, pale is interesting, as touches of warm beige and cooler stone coloring highlight the neutral theme. The beauty of a mainly white scheme is that every addition makes its mark. Subtle textures – quilted fabric, woven wicker, the quiet greens of foliage – all combine here in an attractive, understated way.*

73

NEUTRALS WITH COLOR

Neutral backgrounds or neutral accents usually work hard in a color scheme. Their contribution to visual harmony and tonal balance in a room is sometimes overlooked, but without neutrals there would often be no breathing space between colors and forms. Neutrals can work in much the same way as a plain mat around a print in a frame – to isolate yet enhance a subject, so that you can appreciate it better.

Similarly, a handsome piece of furniture in a neutral color may look splendid set against another flattering neutral shade, but it might look even more impressive against a dynamic color. One successful device for linking colors and neutrals – particularly strong colors – is to introduce a little visual exchange between them. A pale cream sofa against a vibrant yellow wall has more impact if a dash of toning yellow is introduced for pillows or a piping trim, and a touch of cream appears in a picture or painted molding detail.

Neutral schemes also make it easy for you to introduce color as the whim takes you – you can change the colors of a flamboyant flower display to suit the season or your mood; and of course, add easy-to-change color accents with pillows, throws and ceramics.

▶ *Vibrant yellow walls create a dramatic foil for period-style furnishings in neutral shades. Harmonized with palest cream, touches of toning yellow also find their colorful way into accessories – and with details in contrast black, the effect is Classically elegant.*

◀ *White, deep gray-green and rich terra-cotta play on an integrated neutral/color theme. White takes the supporting role here, providing and maintaining a good balance of fragmented color and pattern.*

▼ *In a reversal of roles – you might expect the chair to make the color statement – fresh apple green creates a color note as well as a smooth, matte background for the subtle textures and weaves of the neutral upholstery fabric and natural matting.*

BLACK AND WHITE SCHEMES

As the ultimate non-color scheme, any room decorated with a black and white theme will impress. This dramatic combination suits all kinds of looks – from period elegance to chic, contemporary styles.

Contrast color schemes do not come any bolder than those based on the major neutrals from opposite ends of the tonal scale: black and white.

Opting for such a dramatic combination may take a certain commitment, but the attraction of opposites speaks for itself in terms of style and elegance. There is something about a black and white theme – primarily, a sense of balance, as black recedes and white advances – that flatters classic, period looks as well as avant-garde, minimalist schemes and quieter, more traditional interiors.

The great advantage in choosing a black and white scheme is the absence of color. In an increasingly dazzling and colorful world, it can be a tremendous relief to come home to the tranquillity and sense of order that a black and white scheme offers. Within the scheme you can create striking yet calming balancing acts with expanses of pure black or white, and play subtle visual tricks with pattern and texture, as the eye converts broken black and white to shades of gray. When you do add

▲ *The elegance of Art Deco style and the glamour of the 1920s and 1930s are celebrated in this glossy black and white hall. Shiny chrome and sparkling mirrors, together with the warm, neutral floor coloring enhance a perfectly balanced scheme.*

color to a scheme – for a background or as accent details – the impact is immediate, as black and white enhance and define the unique qualities of each tint and shade.

BLACK AND WHITE BACKGROUNDS

Choosing black or white as a background gives you the equivalent of a blank canvas, so it seems appropriate that many black and white schemes display a precise, graphic quality. They present a fine-tuned sense of symmetry and proportion, where furniture, furnishings and accessories are almost instinctively placed in a formal way to mirror and balance one another.

Whether the scheme is mostly white with a scattering of black accents, or black with splashes of white, both will accentuate the sinuous lines of period furniture and throw more hard-edge, contemporary designs into flattering relief. Other elements in the scheme are highlighted too. Rather as a neutral picture mat provides an eye-calming surround to draw attention to the main subject, a black or white background will place architectural details, soft furnishings and accessories in the limelight.

Jet black and pure white present the strongest contrasts, but there are many softer variations to choose as a starting point, or to use as details within a predominantly black or white scheme. In strongly contrasting black and white schemes, 'less is more', so an uncluttered or minimalist approach to furnishing style and decorations is the most successful – as well as the most dramatic. Charcoal gray and soft, creamy white give the impression of black and white – particularly when an accent color is introduced – and a play of different black and white patterns and textures balanced with neutral wood tones can further soften a potentially stark effect.

A sense of ordered calm is underlined by the simplicity of the layout in this mainly white scheme. Touches of black through the lamps and pillows, and subtle piping on the sofas, guide the eye from the main focal point, the black fireplace.

The graphic qualities of a black and white scheme seem to highlight an instinct for symmetry – the desire to create a pleasing visual balance. The theory is perfectly illustrated here by the mirror imaging of all the major elements in this elegant hallway.

White schemes In a room with plenty of natural light, and where you want to create an illusion of height, you can create an almost ethereal feeling of space with white walls and ceiling, white upholstery and pale-toned flooring. This is a perfect setting for simple, architectural-style features such as a black iron fireplace; a black and white inlay pattern or checkered flooring; a splendid black and white curtain treatment or a handsome piece of black furniture. With these basic elements in place, you can concentrate on providing the finishing touches within the main white setting. Look for fabrics and finishes and complementary shapes in tones and textures of black and white. Introduce these as light fittings, pillows and pictures. Choose accessories and details with streamlined, functional shapes or with ornate curves, as appropriate to the room style.

Black schemes Intense and dramatic, a mainly black room relies on a subtle play of light and texture to create an interesting atmosphere. As black naturally 'pulls in' the size of the room, the best location for a mainly black scheme is a room that can easily take the effect of reduced proportions.

Bathrooms and kitchens, and to some extent, bedrooms, can take a mainly black scheme. In a bathroom and kitchen particularly, there are opportunities to contrast and compare a variety of black surfaces. Shiny tiles, glossy smoked glass and laminates, matte black stone and venous marble effects, black ash wood, fluffy toweling and soft cotton textiles can all contribute a rich mix of black textures and finishes. In a bedroom, you can take a lead from Japanese style, with black lacquered cabinets, screens and cupboards, or furnish with fashionable dark metal furniture. A black, iron-framed bed and coordinating bedside tables and chairs will also enhance a mostly black bedroom scheme.

In a black and white room where every element is carefully chosen for its elegant lines and period interest, warm wood tones provide a neutral, yet visually dramatic, go-between.

A black scheme requires a clever counterbalance of dark and light to create a 'friendly' effect. Here, rich mahogany wood tones and red and gold highlights, together with splashes of pure white, keep the glossy black and charcoal gray stripe scheme looking warm and welcoming.

77

PATTERN AND TEXTURE

To work well, black and white schemes need a good balance of pattern and texture, so take inspiration from the wealth of black and white designs favored by different historical periods. A classic black and white checkered marble floor is an enduring device for defining and enhancing a space, as the geometric patterns create a sense of proportion and perspective. Variations on this check and diamond theme – which suit most room styles – are found in less expensive linoleum and vinyl flooring. Checks of all sorts – from tartan effects to gingham – look good in black and white, especially where the crossover threads give the pattern depth by creating subtle shades of gray.

Black and white stripes are a decorative success in a similar way to checks, and come in as many variations, from humble ticking to satin stripes and wild, almost abstract, zebra stripes. Viewed from a distance, the eye creates its own 'local' shade of gray from the mix of black and white, which again, can be a device you can use to add visual interest to a scheme. Stripes also lead the eye in their direction – a useful ploy if you want to emphasize scale and create a sense of movement.

Dramatically simple, and visually exciting, the scroll patterns in the cast-iron staircase create a lace fan effect against the geometric check floor tiles – only black and white could look quite so effective.

Warm yellow takes any hint of starkness from this classically inspired black and white scheme. It also provides a subtle breathing space between the various pattern elements.

▲ *A delicate black and white toile de Jouy print 'reads' as shades of gray. This creates a subtle link between the dramatic black of the fireplace, the expanse of white wall and the black and white tracery effect of the door paneling.*

Designs derived from classical engravings make a fashionable black and white pattern theme. Often grand and imposing, these images have a marvellous theatricality about them which looks splendid in modern, Dramatic style schemes as well as in more traditional interiors. On a quieter note, toile de Jouy prints – finely drawn figurative designs, which mostly feature pastoral scenes – have a softer, prettier look. These work well in a black and white colorway, in white or gray schemes where their delicate qualities are shown to advantage.

Silhouette motifs, based on positive and negative images borrowed from traditional folk art, also look most effective in black and white. Their influence is often seen in floral-inspired appliqué patterns and in patchwork designs. As accessories – pillows and throws – they add a wonderful, integral pattern splash against solids, stripes or checks.

▲ *Traditional folk art gets an updated image in graphic black and white. The effect is crisp and fresh and strikingly modern.*

BLACK AND WHITE DETAILS

If the drama of a black and white scheme appeals, but creating it seems too big a step to take in one go, try out the effect in measured doses. When you add black and white details, aim for a balance, so that the eye has a focal point and then another point of reference to relate it to. Having two or three elements – lamps, pictures, pillows – will help achieve this harmony.

In a white scheme, or one based on pale neutrals, take the plunge by giving a window treatment a theatrical flourish with bold black and white drapes. Balance the effect with black and white pillows, a throw in matching fabrics, or with touches such as table lamp shades, or an ornate black metal chandelier.

Alternatively, create a low-key look with a formal grouping of black and white prints – copies of old illustrations and architectural details are easy to find, or you could frame black and white photocopies of pictures you like. Mount them in black frames for a classic effect. Black and white details like these look very impressive on colored walls, especially in shades from the historical color palette such as yellow, jade green or deep blue.

▲ *Enhance the timeless appeal of a black and white scheme with prints and engravings of classical themes. Used singly or as a group, they contribute their own subtle range of shades and textures.*

▲ *In a play of textures and metallic accents, soft white provides the background, while matte and silky black sketch in the details. From the feature pillows, to the delicate lines of the bedside chair and the picture arrangement, the eye is engaged by these small but effective touches.*

◄ *Zebra, pony and big cat prints look larger than life, but just as wild, as dramatically different soft furnishings. These patterns work best as black and white focal points in a neutral, minimalist setting.*

▲ *Sumptuous black and white stripes are an inspired choice for drapes, as they accentuate the elegant proportions of a tall window. The impression they create is both classic and dramatically modern in its simplicity.*

HISTORIC ENGLISH COLORS

Whether you are restoring a period home to its former glory, or taking inspiration from a style of the past, there are ready-mixed heritage paints to help you re-create authentic color schemes.

Choosing a pleasant neutral shade of paint from a selection known as 'Common Colors' may sound a bit repellent, but down-to-earth descriptions such as 'Eating Room Red', 'Downpipe' and 'Wainscot' are a feature of Historic English paints, and were originally designed to lead the decorator to the appropriate paint shade for the job in hand.

The equivalents of today's popular neutrals – magnolia, beige and buttermilk shades – were originally derived from relatively inexpensive quarried earth pigments. Consequently, these colors were mainly used in poorer homes and to color 'below stairs' areas in grand houses – passageways and kitchens. The deep color shades of red, blue and green had expensive rare minerals in their makeup, and so were exclusive to the most affluent households. Woodwork was mostly painted in off-white, neutrals or dark brown to imitate expensive hardwood. The one color notable for its absence was brilliant white – this wasn't produced until the 1940s.

When choosing Historic paint colors – in their typically dead flat or soft sheen finish – it is reassuring to know that modern paint manufactur-

Historic colors were often surprisingly bright, providing a dramatic backdrop for sumptuous furnishings. Inspired by the rich tones of the Victorian palette, this period-style dining room recaptures that balance.

ers have developed new ways to interpret traditional formulas. Period paint recipes often contained alarming ingredients. These included lead, arsenic or sulphur, as well as messy binding agents such as egg yolk, rabbit skin glue, wine vinegar and linseed oil. Painting a room has never been easier than it is now.

81

GEORGIAN COLORS

The elegant Georgian period of England, which lasted from 1714-1837, took its inspiration from Italian Neo-Classical architecture. Through the influence of architect Robert Adam, 'Common Color' earth pigment shades of soft white, sand, beige, lead gray and chocolate, used by most of the population, were elevated to grander status to simulate fashionable ancient stone effects in the hallways and staircases of the nobility. Together with 'Adam Green' (a soft sage green), these paler muted colors are typical of the entire Georgian period, and work well in modern neutral schemes.

Throughout the period, the gentler colors – soft reds, pinks, and pale yellow – were often used to decorate drawing rooms. Pale 'Georgian' greens and powder blue were favored for bedrooms, where pattern and stronger color contrast was provided by soft furnishings. By the early 1800s decorations were more adventurous, especially in grander homes, where walls above dado height were painted in bright colors, or covered with wallpaper or fabric. As new pigments were discovered, paler shades made way for expensive, brilliant colors. Strong colors such as 'Kings Yellow' and 'Empire Green' were particularly favored in dining rooms and formal areas.

The texture and soft finish of Historic paints gives them a subtle cast. This makes stronger Georgian colors just as intriguing a choice for bold contemporary schemes as for period-style interiors.

▼ *During Georgian times, vibrant color paints were made from rare and expensive ingredients, hence the name 'Kings Yellow' for this type of brilliant hue, which only the most affluent homes could afford.*

PUGIN COLORS

The eminent architect and designer Augustus Pugin (1812-1852) was a leading figure of the Gothic Revival movement in England. His work is especially memorable for its dramatic use of strikingly bold color; the development of new pigments and paint formulas through chemical synthethis offered marvelous new decorating possibilities. Colors that had previously been expensive or difficult to produce became more readily available. As an enthusiast for this decorating revolution, Pugin did much to popularize the 'new colors'. With their rich intensity and clarity, with names such as 'Bengal Rose', 'Aconite Yellow' and 'Periwinkle Blue', they have enormous contemporary appeal.

▲ Soft reds and pinks are typical of the earth pigments popular during the Georgian period, when they were much favored for their warming influence in the drawing room or study.

➤ *For dramatic impact – especially in a small space – Pugin's vibrant colors are as remarkable today as they were over a hundred and fifty years ago.*

▲ Quiet aqua tones and soft gray-blues would have set the scene for a Georgian lady's sitting room or bedroom. Pattern interest and bolder colors were introduced through drapes and other soft furnishings.

➤ *Known as 'Duesbury Green', Pugin's rich color works well in this disciplined scheme, where bold black and white complement its intensity.*

VICTORIAN COLORS

As color influences changed slowly, the variety of colors associated with the Victorian period (1837-1901) ranges from the elegant Georgian palette, through the rich colors of Pugin, to the turn of the century and the gentler color schemes inspired by William Morris and the Arts and Crafts Movement.

Typical mid-Victorian color schemes were intense and complex – flamboyant wallpapers above contrast paneling, and vivid, contrasting colors above and below the dado rail. Details such as ceiling roses and moldings were highlighted in strong harmonies and contrasts, with woodwork painted in dark tones. Deep, rich colors served to enhance ornate brocade and velvet furnishings and solid wood furniture. These colors were practical too, helping to disguise grime from kerosene lamps, coal fires and tobacco. Of the stronger colors associated with the period – which include purple, olive green, bronze, deep ochre yellow and strong earth tones – dark green and red stand out. Dark green was thought suitable for a drawing room, and powerful red was favored in the dining room, where it was considered an aid to digestion. Red was also regarded as the perfect background for gilt-framed pictures and prints.

Although Victorian looks may be too cluttered for modern tastes, you can take inspiration from the comfortable atmosphere created by their deep, warm color schemes, to create pared-down modern interpretations. A large mirror in a dramatic gilt frame against a vibrant green or red wall, or a bold terra-cotta and muted gold contrast for a wall and dado in a hallway will capture the essence of the style.

▲ In this modern bathroom, a sense of period style is created with a formal display of classical prints and the deep green color scheme so typical of the dramatic Victorian palette.

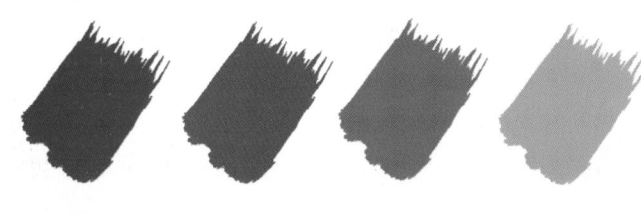

▲ Deep red was a great favorite with the Victorians, especially as a flattering background for gilt-framed paintings and prints. They also chose red to promote a sense of comfortable opulence.

➤ Take a lead from the rich colors of the Victorian age to add vibrant touches in a modern scheme. Here, jewel red and deep green add a period richness to a neutral setting.

WILLIAM MORRIS COLORS

As probably the most prolific British designer, craftsman and decorator of the nineteenth century, William Morris (1834-1896) has left an enduring legacy for furnishing style, pattern and color. Morris was a leading influence within the turn of the century styles – Art Nouveau in Europe and the Arts and Crafts Movement in England. Their design concepts embraced beauty through natural form, craftsmanship and a move from mass production. Morris style is epitomized by flowing stylized floral and figurative textile designs.

Like Pugin, William Morris was an exponent of the new chemically enhanced color palette. With names like 'Quiet Green', 'Half Indigo' and 'Chalk White', his typical color palette is slightly muted – even his dusty red called 'Dragon's Blood Red' is easy on the eye – and well suited to average-size and smaller rooms.

▼ William Morris wallpapers in softly blending colors, such as this large-scale floral and toning leafy design in gentle reds and green, offered an alternative look to Victorian fussiness.

▶ William Morris colors are slightly muted, and typically combined as gentle harmonies or contrasts in his signature, flowing, leafy designs.

EDWARDIAN COLORS

During this short period from 1901-1910, the over-fussy Victorian looks gave way to a lighter, brighter look. The main color influences came from a revival of the paler, early Georgian palette, and the patterns and colors of William Morris, Art Nouveau and the Arts and Crafts Movement. Comfortable looks were still paramount, and many homes now boasted bathrooms with 'modern' white fittings that were enhanced by simpler color schemes.

White paint made with zinc oxide instead of white lead represented a major color breakthrough, as this produced a brighter, more durable finish. White became increasingly popular as a color for woodwork and paneling – typically teamed with soft pinks, blues and lilacs – although darker shades such as ochre, terra-cotta, olive, mid green and brown – were also familiar color combinations.

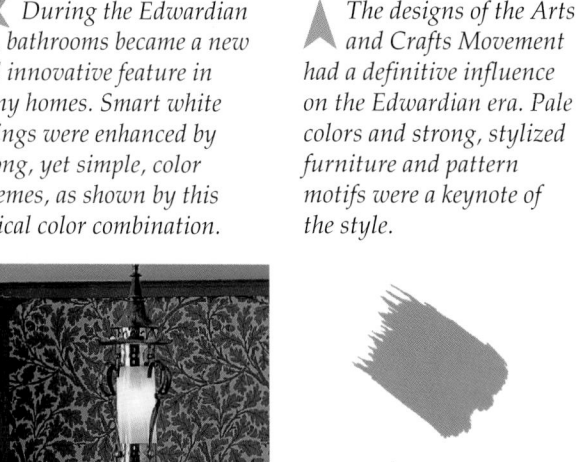

During the Edwardian era, bathrooms became a new and innovative feature in many homes. Smart white fittings were enhanced by strong, yet simple, color schemes, as shown by this typical color combination.

The designs of the Arts and Crafts Movement had a definitive influence on the Edwardian era. Pale colors and strong, stylized furniture and pattern motifs were a keynote of the style.

This turn-of-the-century-style hallway shows how the designs and colors of William Morris, Art Nouveau and the Arts and Crafts Movement influenced the style of the Edwardian home.

AMERICAN COUNTRY COLORS

*Natural vegetable pigments color the American Country
palette, creating the subtle shades that characterize a unique style
based on traditional folk-art motifs and homespun crafts.*

The originators of the folksy but uncluttered American Country style were the early settlers from Europe, who came to the northeastern area of the USA during the eighteenth century. They brought with them a whole wealth of traditional crafts that have become synonymous with the style, as have their typical color schemes.

The colors are recognized by their muted shades of berry red, grayed blue and green, cream and dusty ochre – made from natural earth and plant pigments. Evocative names such as 'Barn red' and 'Cabinetmaker's blue' hint nostalgically at their original settings, while a distinctive soft finish – somewhere between a modern silk or eggshell sheen – gives the colors a subtle patina. These understated colors lend themselves to present-day schemes, where they flatter neutrals and natural themes, and complement simple furnishings in traditional or contemporary settings.

A subtle play of dark and light – notably the pale walls and darker painted woodwork – are typical features of the American Country style. Traditional crafts feature strongly; note the homespun fabrics, a braided rag rug, stenciled folk-art motifs and the punched-paper lamp shades.

AMERICAN COUNTRY LOOKS

There are two main looks and color themes in American Country style: 'Shaker' – named after the religious sect whose philosophy and simple lifestyle focused on creating harmony between form and function, and the patterned style known as 'Pennsylvania Dutch'. This name is a derivation of German *Deutch*, and includes a wide range of folk-art influences from northern Europe and Scandinavia. Stylized motifs of birds, hearts and flowers in soft reds and pinks, greens, blues and off-whites appear in needlework and stencil designs, and in typical American Country patchwork.

Both Shaker and Pennsylvania Dutch styles use a subtle blend of dark and light colors and gently contrasting textures to create a feeling of coziness and tranquility. Capture the look with pale, colorwashed walls that have the feel of bare plaster, using traditional Shaker colors from specialist suppliers, or water-based paints in similar tones. Slightly muted, darker colors for the woodwork are typically American Country, as is an almost matte finish.

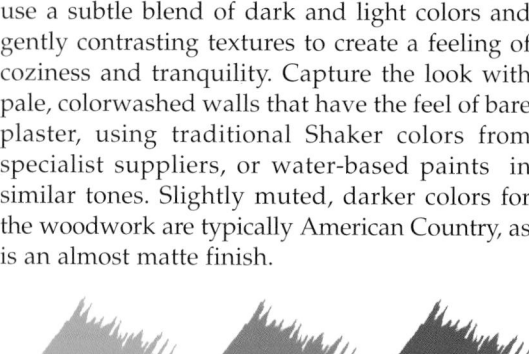

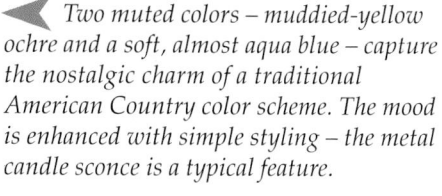

Two muted colors – muddied-yellow ochre and a soft, almost aqua blue – capture the nostalgic charm of a traditional American Country color scheme. The mood is enhanced with simple styling – the metal candle sconce is a typical feature.

‹ 'Cabinetmaker's blue' is a subtle, grayed blue-green, and a familiar hue on the American Country palette. Used for window frames and skirtings, and teamed with soft-white walls, it flatters the mellow tones of polished wood and the metallic accents – typical features of this style.

▲ The subtle contrast of the green colorwashed table against the soft yellow walls is typically American Country, as are the stenciled borders and motifs, and the woven cotton floor runner.

► A refreshing white setting provides a flattering background for an eclectic mix of American Country furnishings and crafts. Warm wood tones and the blue sprig-print sofa create a good tonal balance with the mostly neutral-colored accessories.

COUNTRY COLOR BLENDS

Typical American Country color schemes – especially Shaker-influenced schemes – center on simple, lovingly-crafted furniture and accessories made from mellow beech, maple or cherry. Set against pale, creamy-white or buttery-yellow walls and contrasting, dark-painted woodwork, the effect is complemented by dark metals, such as forged iron light fittings, and the silvery gleam of punched-tin candle-holders and accessories.

Favorite colors for the Shaker's window frames and skirtings, as well as dressers, painted chairs and signature peg rails (furniture and household accessories were all hung neatly from these), are grayed blues and greens, cranberry red and dusty yellow ochre or deep, forest green.

Homespun check fabrics, simple ginghams and braided rag rugs pick up these subtle colors, and blend them with the soft neutrals of warm stone, grayed-beige, moss green and natural white linen.

The American Country style is a look that is easy to borrow from – particularly for small to medium-size rooms. Here, the soft color contrasts can lend definition to architectural features, and help to create a feeling of space.

A balance of light walls and dark woodwork is a traditional feature in American Country color schemes. Here, set against natural white, a dulled red, often known as 'New England red' complements other favorites – shades of soft green.

The warm hardwood floor creates a visual link with the furniture and mellow brick. Muted shades of cranberry red for traditional check fabrics and furnishings, and a soft, green-gray for woodwork – also echoed in the rug – create subtle harmonies and contrasts.

Capture the essence of an American Country interior with 'Barn red' woodwork against soft white walls, a toning sprig-print for curtains, a traditional wooden chair and a needlework sampler.

Create a Shaker effect by fitting a peg rail round the room – painted in an American Country color to match a dado rail, and accessorized with authentic-looking details.

AMERICAN COUNTRY PATTERNS

A distinctive home-grown pattern style has developed from the early American settlers' legacy of treasured possessions and locally made furniture and artifacts. Improvization was their stock-in-trade, as painted and stenciled effects were used to mimic expensive printed wallpapers, and patchwork and appliqué designs aspired to copy multicolor fabric prints. Borrowing heavily from traditional folk-art designs, many of the patterns also had a charming symbolism: the pineapple – seen frequently in traditional patchwork and as a stencil motif – represented hospitality, while hearts and flowers spoke a romantic language.

This naive decorative look has come full-circle, as now you can choose modern stencil-effect wallcoverings, and printing blocks and stamps, to capture the simplicity of traditional American Country motifs. Adopt the theme to decorate walls, fabrics, and simple pieces of furniture such as cupboards and wooden trunks. Furnish with functional fabrics such as gingham, calico and painted canvas floorcloths, and with simple muslin and linen. Add a patchwork quilt or sampler to underline the look.

Bold block patterns are a feature of American patchwork, and the house motif repeated across this bed quilt is a popular image. A mix-and-match approach to design, with stencil patterns, painted scenes and figurative cutouts, all balanced with cream and white, epitomizes the rustic style.

A European heritage of folk art and the influence of Native American crafts are lovingly acknowledged in this country-style bedroom. Stenciled motifs and silhouette designs are typically Pennsylvania Dutch, while the woven blanket and pillow patterns have American origins.

Patchwork and appliqué pillows, made with homespun check fabrics and toning solids, will inject a colorful, American country flavor to a simple setting.

SPICE COLORS

Take inspiration from the subtle tones of ground kitchen spices to create color schemes that are in every way as palatable a blend as their culinary namesakes.

Hearth and home – warming spice colors play their part in conjuring up a comforting, homey atmosphere. Vibrant mustard yellow and hot, but muted chili red set the scene, supported by mellow wood tones, glinting metallic accents and a calming neutral background.

The term 'hot and spicy' tends to make you think of spice colors in the same way as their taste, but in fact, many spice colors are relatively cool, and all are surprisingly subtle – as with cooking, it is the balance that brings out their special qualities. Spice colors certainly offer all the potential their name implies: try using them in a room to promote a warming, mellow feeling; to deliver an exotic touch as backgrounds and rich accent colors, or simply introduce them as a pep-up for soft, neutral schemes.

Subtlety of color mix and tone is the keynote when using spice colors, and this is what makes them such an exciting, adaptable decorating option. As a color group, they range from subtle beiges and cool browns to vibrant yellows and sizzling earthy reds. Most have a tantalizing edge – a second glance often makes you question your first impression. The clear quality of a bright mustard yellow can catch your eye, but on closer scrutiny it could develop a greenish tinge, or perhaps seem slightly brown – just as chili red may in fact turn out as a brownish pink or orange when compared with another red.

When you opt for the richness of a spicy color scheme, it is always worth combining different tones of several spice colors. They harmonize beautifully with one another and blend well with stronger colors. They are also a reliable color backup for neutrals, and classic black and white.

Turmeric yellow provides a vibrant color shot and a unifying background for the various framed subjects. A cleverly placed mirror reflects the touches of green that cool the scheme, and contrast with the pepper-red accents.

MUSTARD YELLOWS

This is really a broad term for a range of muted yellows – as one look at the supermarket shelves will show how varied mustard yellow can be – from the vibrant English type to the muted and grayed or brown-toned German and French varieties.

As a background color, a muted, mustard yellow can be undemanding and restful on the eye. Soft mustard yellows are the easy-to-live-with colors of mellow stone and sand – the natural accompaniment to pale neutral schemes with low-key styling and flattering dark green, leafy accents.

However, when you team these yellows with contrasts, such as muted turquoise, lime green or soft, coral pink, they take on a different quality, with echoes in the classical color schemes of the past, as well as projecting a more contemporary feel. These contrasts look fresh and modern teamed with stream-lined, pale wood furniture, brushed steel and metallic accents, and matte or satin paint finishes.

Used full-strength, English mustard yellow creates a color punch in a largely neutral scheme. Clever touches with the choice of accents – harmonious turmeric yellow, and vibrant, contrast blue – really enhance the potent, yet surprisingly cool quality of this spice color.

CURRY TONES

Turmeric, Madras curry and garam masala are just a few of the so-called curry spices. The brightest of these is golden yellow turmeric and, like saffron yellow, traditionally used for dyeing fabrics. Warm orange-brown curry tones look splendid teamed with cooler earthy shades and neutrals such as stone, as well as with muted brick reds. Used full strength for walls and major furnishings, they are calmed with contrasting cool greens and turquoise, blues and grays. Reduced with white to an almost peachy-apricot or sand, and teamed with pale, cool contrasts such as light gray, mint green or aqua, they still retain a hint of their original strength.

Blending easily with the adjacent warm wood tones, a muted mustard-yellow colorwash elevates a pleasant, yet unremarkable dresser into a real focal point. The toning bold check tablecloth creates a balancing finishing touch.

All the curry spices find their way into this glowing scheme, where warm neutrals tone down the heat. The predominantly yellow coloring promotes a sense of warmth and cheer, while splashes of deep green refresh and provide tonal balance.

WARMING SPICES

As a group, spice colors are more gentle and muted than similar pigment shades. The intensity of earth colors and the vibrancy of mineral pigments is absent, but there is still a richness in these quieter characteristics. This is very noticeable with spice reds. Chili and paprika red have softer qualities than terra-cotta and iron oxides, and this can make them easier to handle in a color scheme. You can also harness their intensity through paint effects, where the mottled effect of broken color – a deeper shade over a clear, paler base coat – can show off the best of these glowing colors.

Even the hottest chili red has a dusty blush to temper its impact. Both chili and softer paprika reds work naturally with warm wood tones, and flatter soft neutrals such as buff and cool brown. For successful harmonious schemes using a group of warm spice colors, simply look at a row of filled spice jars

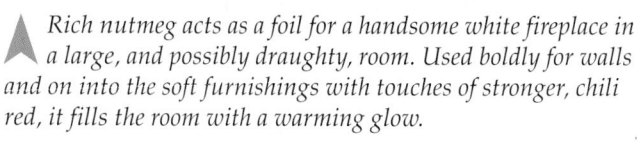

▲ *Rich nutmeg acts as a foil for a handsome white fireplace in a large, and possibly draughty, room. Used boldly for walls and on into the soft furnishings with touches of stronger, chili red, it fills the room with a warming glow.*

▲ *Basing a scheme on a group of close harmonies – in this case spice colors paprika, chili, nutmeg and cinnamon – is a format for a comforting, easy-on-the-eye look. Here, any risk of monotony is relieved by exciting textural details and good tonal balance.*

for inspiration. Vibrant combinations could include chili, paprika and cinnamon, with a dash of nutmeg and a little calming ginger. Use these colors together in any proportions, but balance them with contrast accents and stabilizing neutrals. Green plants, an expanse of dark wood, and glinting metallic touches will flatter warm spice colors and help create a rich, but mellow color scheme.

For a different look, but still with exotic overtones – although the styling can be more contemporary chic than nostalgic spice route – try balancing chili or paprika red with cool turquoise and fresh green, as well as with pinks and apricot. These contrasts are the colors of glowing silks. Or you can tint all the colors with white to become delicate pastels, and still retain something of their spicy origins.

Spice colors have a richness that lends them well to broken color paint techniques, such as sponging, colorwashing and stippling. Here, a curry base color is given extra intensity with a paprika red paint effect. Dark brown details carefully balance the finished effect.

Shades of palest ginger create a unifying, restful background for warming chili and Madras curry stripes and solids in this exotically inspired bedroom. The hand-painted quality of the soft furnishing prints adds to the softness of the color scheme.

MIXED SPICE COLORS

The term describes the traditional cake baking spices of cloves, cinnamon, ginger, nutmeg and cardamom. With the exception of auburn-red cloves, most of these are gentle, soft brown shades. Browns are really versatile decorating neutrals and, as such, are outside the scope of the color wheel. They can be warm or cool, and include muted hues of yellow, orange, red and violet, and make an excellent foil for any strong or vibrant color.

Try teaming mixed spice browns with bright accents and adjacent harmonies – warm acid green through to red – as well as with elegant black and white. Historical color schemes team spice browns with mauve, buff and gold, and they are always flattered by metallic accents of copper, pewter and antique gilt.

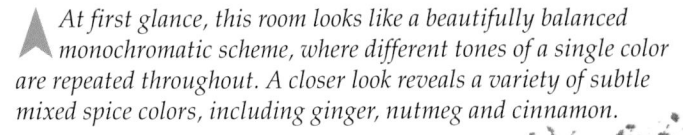

▲ *At first glance, this room looks like a beautifully balanced monochromatic scheme, where different tones of a single color are repeated throughout. A closer look reveals a variety of subtle mixed spice colors, including ginger, nutmeg and cinnamon.*

▼ *Elegant and restrained, muted ginger and cardamom tones blend gracefully with parchment accents in a scheme where subtle textures play an important role.*

▲ *The attraction of color opposites, red and green, is the starting point for this wonderfully rich, clove red hallway, contrasted with black-toned and muted forest green woodwork. A pinch of mixed spice for the floor and stairs adds the essential neutral quality needed to enhance the effect.*

Patterns are everywhere. The most obvious examples are found in fabrics and wallcoverings. More subtle patterns are found in the swirls of wood grain and scrollwork, the stripes of paneling and floorboards and the woven repetition of basketry and rattan. The arrangement of decorating details such as a collection of pictures or a row of books may also create pattern. A pleasing balance of assorted patterns considers their style, scale, use of color and variations of texture and line.

This section clarifies patterns common to home decorating. Some patterns, such as florals and fruits and vegetables, are characterized in various ways to be suitable for different decorating styles. Other patterns, such as animal prints and those having an Eastern influence, are more suitable for dramatic and exotic decorating styles. Stripes, checks and plaids provide an assortment of linear patterns whereas graphic images include historic and naturalistic studies.

DEFINING FLORALS

*Whether your preferences are for traditional, full-blown
cabbage roses, pretty sprig prints or flamboyant brush-stroke blooms
– there are florals to suit all tastes and room styles.*

Selecting a particular floral design, whether for wallpaper or soft furnishings, is rather like choosing real flowers for a special occasion – you know you need to get it right. Striking a balance is very important, not just through your choice of blooms and their colors, but with the size and style of the arrangement – formal or understated, dramatic or romantic.

Floral patterns come in many guises, and generally fall into three groupings – the large-scale, exuberant florals, the medium-scale, more versatile florals and the small and

Contemporary-style florals are perfectly suited to informal soft furnishings. Often freely drawn with a paintbox freshness, their simplicity suits many modern lifestyles.

pretty mini prints. Some florals are highly stylized and barely discernible as flowers, others are as naturalistic as fine botanical studies. You see florals freely strewn across their backgrounds, grouped neatly between stripes or checks or arranged with geometric precision in sprigs.

Some decorative looks are naturally inclined to florals – think of the floral

chintz tradition in English country style, or the typically 'feminine' floral bedroom. Other styles use florals in a less overt way, and in many instances less is more – a bright floral splash for a window blind or duvet cover in a contemporary setting will have as much impact as an all-over floral theme in a period cottage setting.

As a guide to defining florals and a help in choosing them for your own schemes, the floral designs on the following pages show their main characteristics and how different types are naturally suited to particular room styles.

Dramatic Florals

Romantic-style florals can be pretty and feminine – finely drawn with a nostalgic period feel, or stylized, modern and ethereal – printed on fine and sheer fabrics, perhaps with a hint of gold or metallic accents. Usually medium to small scale, they are particularly at home as soft drapes in the bedroom and as lavish, filmy window treatments and coordinating cushion covers in the living room.

Glamour-style florals tend to be formal, but with a flamboyance and color shimmer that singles them out as luxurious and opulent. Seen as self-colored damasks, brocades, and with satin stripes, they rely on tonal shifts rather than a mix of colors for effect. Often seen in rich cream shades, and deeper, intense reds and blues, they suit traditional furnishing styles and window treatments.

CLASSIC FLORALS

Classic-style florals are elegant and refined, often with the quality of fine, period engravings. As large- to medium-scale designs, these florals appear in formal arrangements on chintz and wallpapers, grouped between intricate stripes, and entwined around classical motifs or musical instruments. Their backgrounds are usually cream or pale. Use different-scale florals together in a scheme for formal furnishings: full-length curtains with swags and tails, canopied bed treatments, upholstery and paneled walls.

Period-style florals focus on a particular historical look. To create a turn-of-the-century style, influenced by the rich colors of Victorian and Art Nouveau styles, choose the detailed, flowing florals designed by William Morris for walls and soft furnishings.

ETHNIC FLORALS

Ethnic-style florals draw their inspiration from global sources, with all their diverse influences. Mostly mid- to small-scale, they share a rich color intensity – often a balance of dark and light contrasts – with a linear quality typical of hand blocking, batik and other traditional printing methods. Typical looks are the bold and sumptuous, Eastern and Moorish-inspired florals, combined with intricate geometric shapes and paisley forms. Use these richer patterns where you want to create a feeling of comfort and opulence.

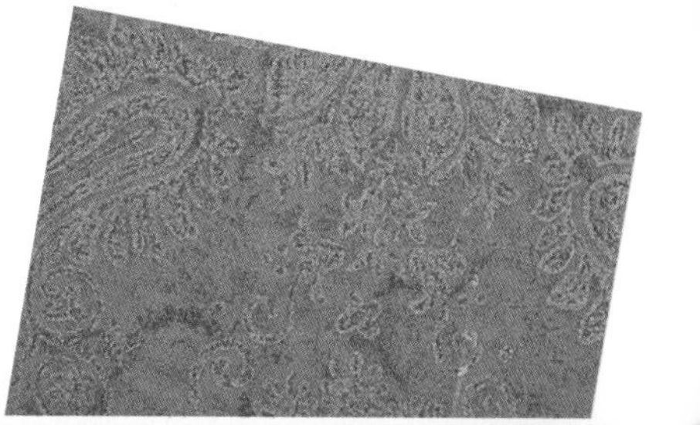

Provençal-style prints are traditional small-scale florals from the south of France. They are typified by vividly colored, busy little sprigs and floral motifs, often with finely drawn black outlines, on white or bold primary color backgrounds. In a sophisticated color combination they look quite 'grown-up', but they are mostly known for their sunny, bright and cheerful image in an informal setting such as a kitchen.

FRUIT AND VEGETABLE THEMES

*Look to the kitchen garden for inspiration, and celebrate its bounty
with a decorative theme of fruit and vegetables. Find them on fabrics
and wallcoverings, and as a whole harvest of accessories.*

Fruit and vegetable designs follow a similar decorative tradition to the more familiar floral themes, but they offer an unusual – and increasingly popular – approach to bringing beautiful images from the garden and countryside into the home.

The shift in appreciation is reflected in the growing number of coordinated items that feature fruit or vegetable themed wallcoverings and soft furnishings. Some even include prettily painted ceramics and accessories, as well as color-matched stripes or checks and toning solids. Take a lead from the way these designs are put together – there is no reason

Colorful contrasts red and green are worked together in a delicious cherry-ripe print – perfect for an informal country look. One of the pleasures of a fruit or vegetable theme is collecting accessories such as these amusing dishes (left).

to limit fruit and vegetable themes to the kitchen – but however you use them, let the patterns play a leading role in the scheme. Bold designs and bright colors mostly love plain backgrounds or fresh white, where they can take center stage. For a low-key scheme that relies more on accessories to set the theme, look for hand-painted fruit and vegetable china, and amusing wood and plastic 'fruit and veg' shaped objects, cutlery and gadgets.

Fruit Designs

Seen on fabrics and wallcoverings, fruits occupy much the same ground as florals – large- and small-scale patterns, naturalistic botanical studies, freely drawn interpretations or stylized motifs. They are as adaptable as florals and, like florals, suit different decorating styles.

A robust vine garland pattern, complete with juicy bunches of grapes and curling tendrils, can have all the grace and energy of a classic-style frieze, while the same subject in a more stylized form may show the hallmarks of the sinuous, turn-of-the-century textiles of William Morris and the Art Nouveau period. Such fruit designs are likely to find their way into period-style living rooms, bedrooms or halls, while a splashy, more abstract grapevine pattern, or a neatly stenciled bunch of grapes motif, is more likely to be seen in a contemporary or country-style kitchen or dining room. However, there are no fixed rules to say what goes where, and an unexpected color or pattern element can work wonders in a room scheme.

➤ *Botanical studies of luscious garden fruits cascade over the bed canopy and create a pretty quilt trim in this delightfully romantic bedroom. A crisp white background and toning soft green flatter and highlight the vivid colors of the fruit.*

◄ *Sharp and cool citrus yellow always looks fresh teamed with green. The lemon tree is one of nature's agreeable color arrangements on the fruit theme and, teamed with crisp white, works very prettily as a fabric print.*

Fruit traditions

Fruit has traditionally played a high profile role in interior and exterior decoration, from typical country-style subjects for stencils, appliqué or patchwork, to elaborate murals and carved embellishments in grand, classical homes. In American country style, the pineapple symbolizes hospitality and, as a favorite fruit motif, appears in many homespun crafts. Pineapples also find their way into English Regency design, seen atop metal column candlesticks and as table lamp and stone table bases.

With their bright, cheery image, summer fruits – cherries, strawberries and other berries – look appealing as simple, almost childlike designs, especially when drawn with clear, graphic outlines over fresh, pale or white backgrounds. The sharp yellows, greens and oranges of citrus fruits have a special impact too, which is particularly effective in designs worked in a naturalistic or botanical study style.

Use clearly defined images as feature patterns for window blinds and curtains in kitchens, dining rooms and conservatories where the play of light will enhance their coloring and detail, and for tableware or feature wallcoverings. Atmospheric 'tropical' designs, featuring exotic fruits and berries, often provide strong images and outline shapes, which are perfect for making fun placemats and appliqué tabletop accessories.

umans Reinette.

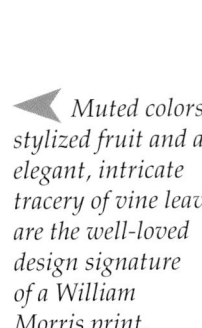

▶ *Imaginative solutions to everyday tasks, and a re-think on familiar shaped objects, has led to the development of the potted cactus lemon squeezer.*

◀ *Muted colors, stylized fruit and an elegant, intricate tracery of vine leaves are the well-loved design signature of a William Morris print.*

107

VEGETABLE DESIGNS

There is often a humorous element to designs featuring vegetables, especially on fabrics and wallcoverings. The joke is in the sudden realization that the attractive pattern strewn over the cotton chintz is not flowers or fruit, but bunches of radishes, leeks or root vegetables. An unexpected twist can be very endearing, and positively charming.

In decorative terms, the humble cabbage has, until fairly recently, been a poor substitute for a cabbage rose – although cabbages and most fruit and vegetables have traditionally played an inspirational role in ceramic ware. Many contemporary interior designers and florists now regularly raid the kitchen garden for innovative display material to use alongside more conventional accessories, blooms and foliage. A fashionable interest in beautifully drawn botanical studies, and a nostalgia for old-fashioned seed packets with their delicately illustrated specimens, has also awakened a whole new interest in vegetable images as home furnishings.

The obvious place to display vegetable

Vegetable shapes and botanical studies have fascinated ceramic designers for many years; arranged as a repeating image, they have a charm that is all their own.

Underline a country-style cottage theme with pretty vegetable print curtains. Again, a pale background highlights the motifs.

Look again and you see smiling, dancing vegetables – what nicer way could there be to brighten a kitchen than with a sense of humor and appealing vegetable furnishings?

108

print fabrics and wallcoverings is in the kitchen, but, in the right style and on appropriate materials, you can use them in any room in your home.

As with any pattern, team vegetable designs with toning solids or discreet color-coordinated patterns, but try taking the theme a little further. Think of the textures you can use to enhance the theme. Being so close to the kitchen garden, coarse hessian fabrics, weathered wood, terra-cotta pots, mossy-trimmed plant pots, pebbles and simple styling provide appropriate backup for an attractive rustic theme. Alternatively, why not elevate prints featuring luxury vegetables, such as asparagus and artichokes, to a status befitting their place on the culinary ladder, and celebrate this with dramatic or luxurious window dressings, uphol-stery, or beautifully framed collectors'-style prints?

When art imitates life so successfully, spotting the real thing can be a challenge. Creating an arrangement on this theme can be very rewarding, as so many designers and craftsmen find interest in the same subject.

Make a vegetable arrangement the centerpiece for a summer lunch party, or create one as an imaginative alternative to a flower display in a country-style living room or kitchen.

109

THEMED ACCESSORIES

Fantastically detailed, porcelain cabbage, artichoke and pumpkin tureens, and other vegetable-shaped platters and containers on leaf-shaped bases are much sought-after collectables, while less expensive ceramics, hand-painted with citrus fruits or brightly colored vegetables, have a cheerful, Mediterranean look. Other popular ceramic decorations include botanical studies of fruit, and simple, sponge-stenciled fruits and vegetables.

Look for themed accessories for children such as fruit-shaped coat hooks, friezes, or boxes that feature a favorite fruit or vegetable; oversized fruits make perfect motifs for pillows and appliquéd bed linen.

For a touch of country style, decorate table linen with stamped, stenciled or embroidered motifs of cherries, grapes or other fruit. Worked on crisp white linen in cross-stitch or satin stitch, and with blue or red thread, they evoke nostalgic Scandinavian style.

Nothing is too small a subject for a fruit theme treatment. The little gadgets hanging from the banana hook are actually measuring spoons.

Sponge-stenciled fruits look charmingly rustic on everyday tableware. With their subtle, broken coloring, it is easy to mix and match them with toning solid pieces and table linen.

The sheer variety of fruit and vegetable shapes and colors makes them a marvelous subject for character candles. Use them for alfresco eating and lighthearted accessories.

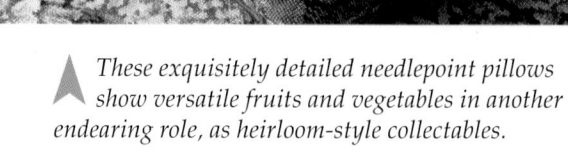

These exquisitely detailed needlepoint pillows show versatile fruits and vegetables in another endearing role, as heirloom-style collectables.

110

ANIMAL PRINTS

Exotic and indulgent, flamboyant and glamorous – animal print furnishings have an image of unashamed luxury. They can also add unique pattern interest to low-key modern settings.

Exotic animal prints and movie star glamour have a time-honored link – a certain celebrity status has long been associated with extravagant furnishings in fabulous big cat patterns, dramatic zebra stripes or reptile motifs. Sofas or chairs covered with a lavish pattern of leopard spots or tiger stripes will always be a focus of attention – it is an irony that although these patterns work as nature's camouflage in the wild, they become eye-catching focal points in a domestic setting.

The modern ranges of animal prints, however, take a tongue-in-cheek look at old-style glamour, by introducing wilder-than-wild fun fur designs based loosely on authentic animal patterns as well as sophisticated and restrained prints in subtle colorings. Sometimes the shades follow nature closely, and sometimes the designs evolve to create exciting effects that give only a passing nod to their animal inspirations. Whether you want to create a romantic safari theme, or a setting where nature's patterns are counterbalanced by modern design, there are animal prints and their many variations to set whatever scene you desire.

Inspired by the glowing colors of the savannah and the intricate patterns of tiger, leopard, cheetah and giraffe, these furnishings show how, used with careful coordination, an animal print theme can be vibrant and modern, with an almost understated elegance.

111

USING ANIMAL PRINTS

Because of their high-profile looks, animal prints are always going to appeal to the extrovert. For anyone who wants to make a dramatic and glamorous style statement, these are the designs to choose. With their very definite looks, big animal prints are obviously impressive. Their strong, often contrasting coloring also means that a little goes a long way, so you need to balance their proportions to avoid a style overdose.

You can just as effectively use these prints for small accessories and details, as for bolder pattern statements. Some animal prints are relatively inexpensive, while others are in the luxury range, so plan accordingly, and save the most luxurious for impressive details.

Try mixing and matching animal prints. By using different scale patterns together you create a lively interest, and the subtle contrasts between the various pattern mark-ings can positively enhance the scheme. To avoid an overwhelming look, keep to a pattern theme with harmonious coloring, such as a blend of warm, honey-toned big cat prints, with perhaps a dash of giraffe for easy color coordination. Because of their strong impact, zebra and black and white animal prints generally work best on their own, or with smaller scale prints in neutrals dark brown and gray, and as mini-prints that echo touches of black or white.

The easiest way to introduce an animal print theme is against a back-ground of warm colors. Use the prints for fabulous upholstery fabrics or impressive paint effects on small-scale pieces. The mostly warm neutral tones of the prints lend them-selves well to other neutrals – soft beige, browns, gold or cream – as well as to vibrant contrasts such as fuchsia pink, hot orange, deep green, and black and white.

As a glamorous style statement, a leopard print sofa is hard to beat. In this contemporary setting, an elegant lamp with giraffe-like proportions creates an understated, humorous foil to the sleek lines of the big cat sofa.

Choosing a style

Big cat patterns and zebra stripes look marvelous in controlled splashes – especially as soft furnishings teamed with rather grand furniture styles. This theatrical effect is best exploited by teaming the prints with period-style pieces – favorite combinations are antique white and gilt or dark wood. Or try the prints with sinuous, contemporary designer styles and smooth, shiny metals, where the hard and soft effects make an interesting contrast. Other styles that work well are simple African or tribal themes, where the emphasis is on natural materials: jute or coconut matting flooring, earthy colorwash paint effects and sturdy, rustic furniture.

A modern, wild-at-heart scheme is celebrated with a liberal use of panther, leopard, cheetah, zebra and snakeskin prints in subtle black, white and gray. These are complemented by fresh green walls and fuchsia, violet and bright blue color accents. Hot earth flooring hints at the scheme's African roots.

Looking remarkably docile as elegant trims on cool cotton sheets, honey-colored big cat prints add a stylish finishing touch to plain bed linen.

Bring the Kenyan plains to your living room with a giraffe-effect table-top. This witty design is painted onto raffia fabric and teamed appropriately with zebra and panther accessories.

Choosing a leopard print carpet takes a lot of nerve, and certainly shows total commitment to the theme. Here the effect is balanced and enhanced by an expanse of neutral cream.

113

ANIMAL PRINT DETAILS

If you would like to use animal prints as accessories and details, rather than backgrounds or main furnishings, then you have many options. As an endearing theme, these prints appear on many ready-made items, ranging from pillows and throws to lamp shades, ceramics and stationery. A tiger stripe screen, zebra print rug or a couple of storage boxes or frames covered with faux leopard paper will create interesting focal points and liven up a simple color scheme.

> *Tiger stripe, cheetah spot and jazzy zebra pillows are guaranteed to create a new decorative look in the quickest possible way.*

Based loosely on animal print patterns, the design on this hand-painted wastebasket echoes the rich earth colors of Africa.

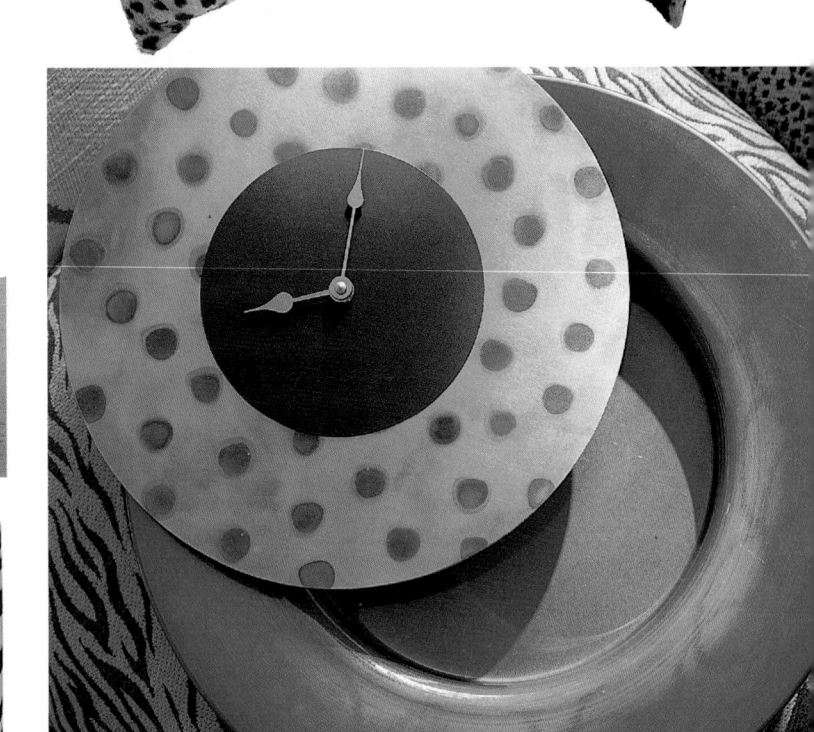

Whether you are going on safari as a serious theme, or just fancy a few animal print accessories, it is the clever little touches such as this cheetah spot clock that hold a look together.

Complement an animal theme with ceramics to match, or create a striking contrast to neutral and vibrant solid color schemes with everyday items in an exotic mix of faux prints.

STRIPES

*From formal Regency stripes or cheap and cheerful ticking,
through jaunty deck-chair stripes to fragmented floral bands –
stripes provide a flexible option for many decorating schemes.*

Stripes have long played an important role in interior design. Applied as painted borders, woven into textiles – formal satin stripe damasks, colorful ethnic rugs and fabrics – as well as printed in countless variations, they have become a classic decorative tool with a tried-and-true pedigree.

You can use the optical tricks that stripes perform to alter the proportions of a room: vertical stripes lead the eye upward to effectively 'add height', and horizontal stripes widen, to 'lower' a tall feature. Stripes can also create a visual breathing space between patterns in a scheme, as their orderly lines provide a link between plain colors and more robust patterns. You can use stripes boldly to provide useful splashes of accent color and detailing in a room, or to create a themed scheme, where stripes are used every which way to maximize their potential as distinctive patterns.

▲ *Informal, gaily striped table linen has a positive 'rise and shine' factor, one to capitalize on in a busy kitchen or family dining room. Team robust stripes with toning crockery and other colorful details for dramatic impact.*

Cool and calm, pure cotton bed linen and accessories in a carefully balanced blend of fine blue and white stripes complement the studied, low-key and natural look of this contemporary-style bedroom.

NARROW STRIPES

Narrow stripes can be the barely-there patterns; in pale or strong tones they create a subtle, broken color effect, so useful as a backdrop for deeper solids or toning patterns and florals. As wallcoverings, use narrow stripes to provide a muted all-over pattern to team with dainty sprig prints, or to balance a stronger toned solid or patterned dado.

Very narrow stripe fabrics such as versatile ticking have an attractive graphic quality that goes well with many contemporary, low-key, furnishings. Here you can play on these subtle qualities with a mixture of different-color stripes, and by making a feature of details such as mitered borders, where stripes match at corners to form right-angled patterns. Use narrow stripes also as diagonal stripe bindings or as patchwork-style blocks, playing visual tricks with vertical and horizontal stripes. These directional variations look particularly attractive set alongside strong toning solids, and incorporated into table or bed linen designs, or teamed with the stripe in its original version.

Exuberant stripes are perennial favorites, giving an instant lift wherever they appear. Here a mix-and-match selection in bright blue and yellow creates a jaunty feeling.

116

◀ On a bold striped theme, horizontal lines of the red and white bed linen balance vibrantly with the contrasting stripes of the blue shutters and the black bed frame.

Stripe effects

Use stripes to complement distinctive 'stripey' features that already exist in a room. Ready-made stripes include the lines of polished or painted floorboards, tongue-and-groove paneling, symmetrically placed windows, or other striped elements such as slatted blinds and iron-framed furniture.

BROAD STRIPES

Broad stripes make a bold statement; even in pale colors and small amounts they display an appealing, extrovert quality. With their lighthearted associations – deck-chair stripes, regatta stripes, circus stripes – they are dashing wherever you choose to use them.

Broad stripes inset with narrower bands and textured or paint-effect stripes have real impact. Balanced carefully in a scheme so as not to overpower, and worked in chalky colors or vibrant brights, they create an immediate focal point, as well as providing an imposing backdrop for bold and neutral solids.

You can customize stripe designs to fit any space, and broad stripes are some of the easiest to work with. Use them to create a dado or to emphasize the proportions in a really small room, by transforming it into a 'tent'. Children particularly appreciate this creative approach.

▶ Creating an optical illusion is easy with bold stripes; here, bright yellow paints a sunny scheme complete with a tented ceiling.

PATTERNED STRIPES

Designs comprising stripes and bands of floral or other motifs are often found as part of coordinating fabrics and wallcoverings. Elements from a main theme arranged together in this way can be a useful decorative device. These patterned stripes introduce a change of pace into a scheme without the color or pattern risks that an unrelated design could pose. The designs might be subtle, elegant and almost self-colored, or gloriously vibrant. Use them in carefully balanced amounts – for dados, for a window blind or curtains balanced with a toning blind, for bed linen or covers on sofas or chairs. With these stripes, the maxim 'less is more' applies.

▶ *Brush-stroke flowers and leaves worked as informal stripes look fresh in green and white, and offer a new slant on familiar florals.*

◀ *Brightly patterned chalk-mark stripes follow a style trend for flamboyant colors and informal florals. Dominant designs such as these are always best used as part of a total coordinating look.*

SURPRISE STRIPES

Sometimes bands of patterns merge or the linear qualities of the stripes change. Nature provides a perfect example with animal stripes. The fragmented lines of zebra stripes, glorious big cat stripes and subtle snakeskin markings inspire many interior designs.

Introduced to a scheme alongside plains, patterns or other, more formal stripes, these broken stripes can look dramatically exotic or provide a subtle, visual double-take, depending on your decorative approach.

In a room decorated exclusively with a coordinating collection, two of the printed designs are, typically, stripes. The floral stripes on the walls and the abstract stripes on the chair seats provide an almost formal note to balance the scattered florals on curtains and tablecloth.

Stars and stripes – in this case animal stripes – give an original twist to a familiar pattern combination. Star motifs in a formal arrangement provide the main stripe detail, which contrasts cleverly with background bands of diagonal, fragmented tiger stripes.

Hot pinks and zingy tangerine combined with cooling neutral beige create a glowing collection of mix-and-match stripes. Designed for bed linen, these cheerful stripe variations would look good teamed with simple, colorwashed walls and toning solids.

Stripe Accents

Stripes in all their variations offer great opportunities as color and pattern accents, especially in neutral or quietly understated schemes. Here, a few well-chosen stripes for soft furnishings and accessories can tip the balance favorably if the room is in danger of looking dull.

In a formal setting, such as a Classic-style dining or living room, the elegant lines of color-woven Regency stripes come into their own. In traditional or avant-garde colors, use them for swags and tails, upholstered chair seats or simply a smart group of pillows.

Brighten up a bathroom with towels, a blind or accessories in snappy stripes, or cheer up a kitchen with banded china and colorful striped table linens. For a bedroom introduce subtle self-color satin stripes for bed linen or choose crisp cotton stripes for a fresh look. Wherever you are adding stripe accents, be aware of any other subtly occurring stripes in the room, so that your choices maintain a pleasing balance.

Capitalize on the potential of vertical and horizontal stripes by turning them into geometric designs. A simple square pillow is a perfect showpiece for a clever stripe idea.

As an informal summer cover-up, or as a key piece in a relaxed-style decor, a striped slipcover will make the sofa a natural focal point.

In a room bursting with rich color, the subtle arrangement of various striped elements is a lesson in understated elegance. Note how the lines of the chair cover, the vertical and diagonal lines of the fireplace border and mirror frame all complement one another.

For a nostalgic country-cottage look, traditional striped pottery has an unmatched charm. Add a few bright pieces as color accents to shelves or a dresser, for an eye-catching play of vertical, horizontal and diagonal stripes.

CHECKS

With a versatility that belies their simplicity, checks are a valuable decorating tool. They work well on their own or with other patterns, and always have their own distinctive style.

Checks – patterns based on crisscross lines and simple geometric grids – come in many guises. All are immensely adaptable. You can find checks and check effects to use on almost any surface in your home – walls, floors, furniture and accessories. They come in a variety of different scales and color combinations to suit almost any decorating style or look.

The simplest checks are created from two different color thread groups woven alternately at right angles to each other – clean and crisp ginghams are this type. As the bands of color interweave, new color effects are created. It is these subtle shades and the potential offered by weaving more colors together in this way that make check designs so versatile and interesting – think of jewel-bright Madras plaids and colorful tartans.

 *Simple checks take on a very grown-up look in this sophisticated bedroom, where the unusual color scheme adds to their appeal. The subtle mix of checks with solids, bold floral stripes and a finely drawn print shows how accommodating checks can be.*

When checks are printed rather than woven, there are even more design possibilities. Checks often appear worked into patterns with florals, stripes, abstracts or figurative motifs, as textiles, wallpapers and ceramics. You can also create check effects with solid colors and textures; think of floor and wall tile arrangements and painted check effects. With their seemingly infinite variety, checks really offer many easy-to-use options.

WORKING WITH CHECKS

Whether they are bright and bold in a snappy, contemporary way, or small-scale and low-key, checks have a refreshingly unpretentious impact. Their ordered simplicity seems to ground them in a scheme, whether they are making a style statement in their own right, or providing a hardworking color and balance link between different pattern elements.

Check designs are always evocative. There was a time when checks meant gingham and were consigned to the kitchen or were the reserve of nostalgic rustic styles. However, modern color mixes take checks much further. Cool blues and soft yellow cotton checks suggest mellow Scandinavian style, while checks in stronger muted shades and cheerful earth tones evoke homespun American Country and Exotic styles. More complex checks, in vibrant multicolor silks, or linen mixes in fashionable color combinations, make another kind of style statement, as do schemes based on mix-and-match multi-checks. Whatever their style, from country to urban chic, the fascination of working with checks owes much to their simplicity and the fact that you can readily incorporate them into most schemes, as the mood takes you.

In this sunny citrus scheme, the toning check pillows provide important pattern interest where curvy shapes, solids and textures take the lead. Like all good checks, their presence is polite and never loud.

In a simple color scheme where bold shapes and clean lines are paramount, bright blue and white checks – for sofa, blinds and floor – create a balanced contrast with mustard yellow highlights.

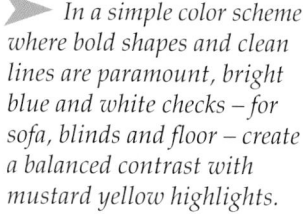

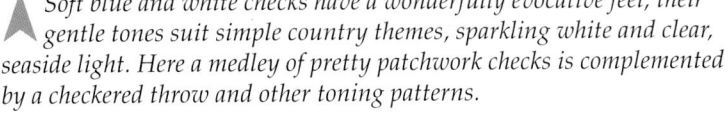
Soft blue and white checks have a wonderfully evocative feel; their gentle tones suit simple country themes, sparkling white and clear, seaside light. Here a medley of pretty patchwork checks is complemented by a checkered throw and other toning patterns.

Practical checks

You can use checks in a scheme rather as you would use neutrals – to create a calming visual bridge between other pattern elements or areas of plain color. Checks share this advantage with stripes and, like them, their regularity can be a stabilizing factor in a scheme, while contributing their own subtle pattern interest. Checks are also a good choice in areas where you would like to use a pattern, but don't want to be committed to a restricting design. Introducing a single check or combining a selection of different size checks can be a very successful alternative.

Checks have many other practical uses, especially small-to-medium-size checks. From a short distance their colors appear to merge to create a mid tone between the main colors of the design. You can use this broken color quality to disguise uneven wall surfaces effectively, soften the lines of furniture and provide camouflage for potential grubby marks and heavy-wear areas.

You can also use checks to help define shapes and accentuate perspective. Checkerboard tiled floors and walls have an enduring appeal for this reason. Think of the classic combination of black and white tiles – the visual effects are quite different depending on whether the checks are set square to the base shape or placed diagonally. When square, a check floor will emphasize the area shape and, if the checks include the wall color, help to create a feeling of space; diagonal lines of checks, however, can seem to 'run away', and so are often used to add visual length to an area.

Gingham checks in two different sizes look crisp and neat twinned for simple bed linen or pillows. The matching covered buttons add a pretty finishing touch.

CHECK VARIATIONS

Many ready-made coordinating fabrics and wallcoverings include checks as a basic option. Checks perform a reliable double act with more vigorous designs such as large-scale florals, and can work visual wonders with matching colored stripes and solids. Bold check designs can lend weight to a scheme; use them on a dado below toning stripes, a floral or a bold solid, or as a border design to strike a balance between plain and patterned areas. The same format, using paler shades, works in just the same way, but with a softer result. Similarly, a large check used for an impressive pair of full-length curtains will accentuate the window shape and counterbalance strong, solid-color walls or upholstery. You can complement the theme by adding pillows or a throw in the matching check.

Multicolor checks and tartan effects, either woven or printed as vibrant brush-stroke grids, are a colorful option for less permanent furnishings such as table or bed linen. Worked over a fresh white background as part of a color-coordinated or neutral theme, or chosen in colors to blend with other patterns and solids in the room, they offer a quick and easy way to add vitality to a scheme.

Painted checks and multi-checks can be as bold or discreet as you choose. Simple block print checks using a sponge make an attractive border along a skirting, behind a work top, or to highlight door panels. You can also use a paint roller or brush to create informal checks across any smooth, flat surface, such as walls, floors or accessories.

Tartan-inspired, or multi-checks, offer a clever way to coordinate different color elements in a scheme. Used as a bright splash for bed linen, these checks tone with the solid elements and introduce a strong pattern without being fussy.

Color coordinates make it easy to combine different patterns. Checks blend happily with stripes and solids when they share a mutual color palette.

A classic way to coordinate checks in a scheme is to lift a color or two from the checks to use as plain accents. These pillows work well in this subtle, understated way.

▶ *Use check patterns to provide a valuable pattern link between florals and color brights. As part of a mix-and-match group of wallpapers and fabrics, checks help balance a wide range of design options.*

▲ *As a general rule for easy coordination, follow through a color theme when mixing checks with other checks. Here, multi-check panels add interest to toning check pillows.*

125

CHECK DETAILS

A single sofa or chair, boldly upholstered in a bright check, will take pride of place in a low-key setting or sit snugly against a richly toning patterned or solid background. A few check details – such as trims and accessories – will also help to liven up a dull room or create a change of balance and a new focus in a patterned scheme. On plain curtains, a simple check fabric for ties or tab headings and bindings will create a whole new look, as will crisp gingham borders on plain bed linen or towels. Checks look good in sharply pressed pleats – make a simple pleated check lamp shade to coordinate with pillows in the same check, or insert a pleated check frill edging on plain pillows or curtain tiebacks.

Look for painted check accessories to complement a plain, stripe or floral theme. Ceramics, tableware, wooden boxes and frames are often available with checkerboard designs, or you can decorate them yourself.

Because they are so versatile, checks work equally well in quiet ways or used as small color splashes. Understated neutral/natural check accessories will do much to enhance a scheme based on subtle solids and textured neutrals. However you use them, checks will have an impact, so you can achieve a lot with just a few check details.

Working through a color theme – in this case navy blue and white – is always interesting when patterns and textures are cleverly balanced. Here, the check theme is echoed not only through the picture mats, but also through the shapes of the frames.

Houndstooth checks are a design classic; more familiar for jackets and skirts, but equally smart on a well-dressed sofa.

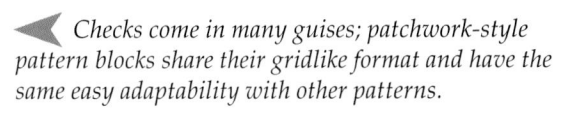

Checks come in many guises; patchwork-style pattern blocks share their gridlike format and have the same easy adaptability with other patterns.

Use check painted ceramics to add a dash of pattern flair in a simple scheme. Choose checks in colors picked out from the main theme, or as accents for a neutral scheme.

TARTAN AND PLAID

*The confident patterns and glowing colors of the Scottish clan tartans
are an enduring feature in home furnishings. You can find them on
just about any surface, from carpets to cups and saucers.*

*A mixture of calm heathery tones and the soft textures
of plaid throws make a welcoming and restful bedroom
scheme. Tartan has a natural alliance with the rich tones
of dark polished wood and rattan.*

Familiar to most people in the form of cozy car rugs, the classic grids and checks woven into traditional tartans originally enabled the Highlanders of old to identify each other in the mists of the moors and mountains, especially in battle. A plaid was a length of strong, twill-woven wool tartan, worn as a kilt by day and used as a blanket at night when out on the hills – hence the connection with traveling rugs. Each clan had its own pattern, with different versions for each occasion – a dress tartan, hunting tartan, and so on.

Queen Victoria made the designs popular and they were loosely copied, using synthetic dyes instead of the original vegetable ones, so that today the term 'tartan' is used to cover a wide variety of grid and block patterns. The tradition and sense of history remain, and for the romantic, a plaid throw or a tartan-covered pillow can still conjure up images of highland crags and heather moors.

With the popularity of checks of all kinds in interiors, tartan is sure to continue its high profile in the home, bringing a cozy warmth and flashes of vibrant color wherever you use it.

TARTAN TRANSLATIONS

Because of tartan's enduring popularity, its general look has been extended into other textiles. You can find the designs woven in light cottons, velvety chenille and even lustrous silk taffeta, in a rainbow of colors, to use just about everywhere. For example, bed linen printed with rich tartan designs is popular for a relaxed, natural look combined with old pine and brass.

The tartan tide is not restricted to fabrics alone – the look now extends all around the home, so it's easy to introduce just a touch of tartan, or use it wall to wall. A richly colored tartan carpet lends a wonderful warm look to a traditional hall. You can find wallcoverings that faithfully reproduce the original pattern, or that interpret the theme so subtly, you would hardly recognize them as tartan, yet they will create a gentle rhythm around the room. Use tartan tiles in your kitchen or bathroom, to provide a splash of vigorous pattern.

For small touches of vibrancy and warmth, choose tiny red tartan candle shades for wall sconces; set a breakfast table with cheerful tartan-painted china; brighten up your bathroom with tartan towels; or accent the top of plain calico curtains with neat bows of narrow tartan ribbon.

Match the rounded petals and rich colors of a bunch of roses with the austere lines of a tartan pot for a simple but surprisingly striking effect.

Translated into bed linen, tartan turns calm and cool in rose pink and sky blue. The strong grid designs are easy to find on china to match your scheme.

Interpreted in a rich taffeta fabric and a sophisticated colorway, tartan makes a grand statement in an elegant town dining room, creating satisfying contrasts with the stone flags, cast-iron candlestick and damask-covered walls.

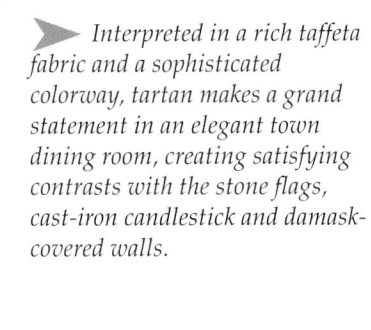

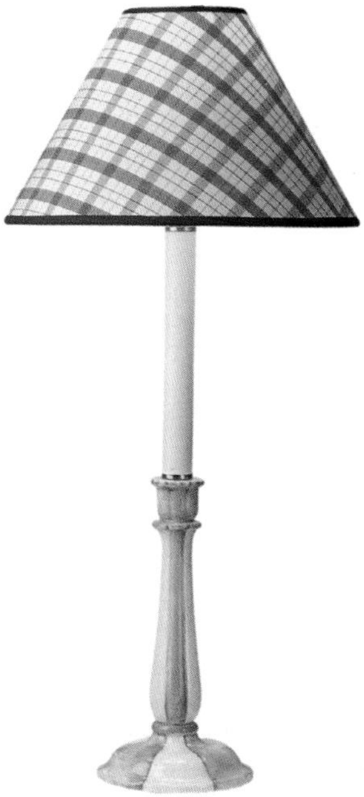

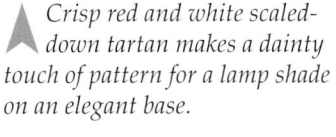

Crisp red and white scaled-down tartan makes a dainty touch of pattern for a lamp shade on an elegant base.

Cheery tartan mugs hung against a split log wall are accentuated with tiny bows of tartan ribbon – a touch you can copy around your home, on candelabra, curtain tops or picture frames.

Fresh and breezy for a summer lunch, choose green and white tartan napkins and rings to brighten up a plain white tablecloth.

PERFECT PARTNERS

Surprisingly, you can mix tartan patterns very successfully with other patterns, to produce lively and interesting combinations. The rigid lines and solid framework of tartan make a flattering contrast to the organic curving shapes of floral and leaf patterns; choose closely related colorways, and intermingle the two fabrics in pillows on a plain sofa, or use tartan as a basis for a rich floral needle-point panel.

Perhaps because of their shared Scottish heritage, paisley and tartan have a natural partnership; try a paisley shawl in soft purples and pinks draped over a chair upholstered in heather and green tartan. Many small woven motifs work well beside tartan, without detracting from the impact of the tartan in the scheme. With their rich, vibrant colors and busy patterns, Provençal prints can match tartan for strength, and the colorways are often close to those in tartans – strong reds, greens and yellows are typical – so they make for a lively but toning mix.

The traditional charm of tartan and lace is cleverly exploited for an original child's bedroom. Dainty lace pillows show up prettily against fresh and cheery tartan wallcovering with a whimsical doggy border; the colors are picked out more strongly in accessories.

The vibrant colors of Provençal cornfields cover a small chair, the repeating motif contrasting strongly with the solid blocks of color in the soft tartan throw. A needlepoint pillow adds crunchy texture.

The bold choice of tartan to partner a huge swirling floral pattern pays off in a double contrast. The rich red of the tartan brings out the warm tones in the floral fabric, while the crisp grid of lines emphasizes the neatly tailored, boxy shape of the sofa, in contrast to the flowing folds of the curtain and cloth.

GRAPHIC IMAGES

Finely drawn motifs and naturalistic studies have long been a favorite decorative device. You can find them in classical or contemporary mood – on fabrics, furnishings and accessories.

Graphic images – those designs and illustrations drawn with an eye to detail and accuracy, portray their subjects with a verve and versatility that can make them witty, romantic, dramatic, imposing or exotic – depending on their theme and character.

Because the subject matter is so varied, there are graphic images to suit all kinds of room style. Part of the fascination for this type of design is its surprise value. A trompe l'oeil design of playing cards on curtains, crockery illustrations on an armchair or a sample of calligraphy across a piece of furniture or a pillow all catch the eye with their gentle humor. These images can prompt a furnishing re-think; used with restraint, they offer an alternative to more familiar surface patterns such as florals and geometrics and give you an inspirational starting point for a decorative theme.

▲ *Classical prints pasted to a bright yellow background were a favorite decorative device of the Georgian era, when special 'Print Rooms' were devoted entirely to this graphic theme. Here, an elegant screen decorated in period style is complemented by the graceful lines of modern furniture.*

131

GRAPHIC THEMES

Seen on wallcoverings and soft furnishings, graphic images of figurative subjects and everyday items have a definite visual impact. Their unexpected appearance in furnishings elevates them into conversation pieces – 'character' prints that are guaranteed to bring a touch of individualism to a scheme.

Although you can use these designs in the same way as other patterns – teamed with plains, neutrals or stripes and checks – the singularity of the images often means that a little goes a long way. Don't be tempted to overstate your point by using the design too freely in a scheme. Depending on the room size and the scale of the images, limit them to key areas, and balance them with blocks of matching/toning plain color and coordinates. One eye-catching character print made into a window blind has more impact in a plain scheme than if used more freely, where it could lose its impact. Think of making a big statement – a dramatic curtain swag or sofa cover – then balance it with toning plains or with a coordinating print on a lamp shade or pillow, or other accessories.

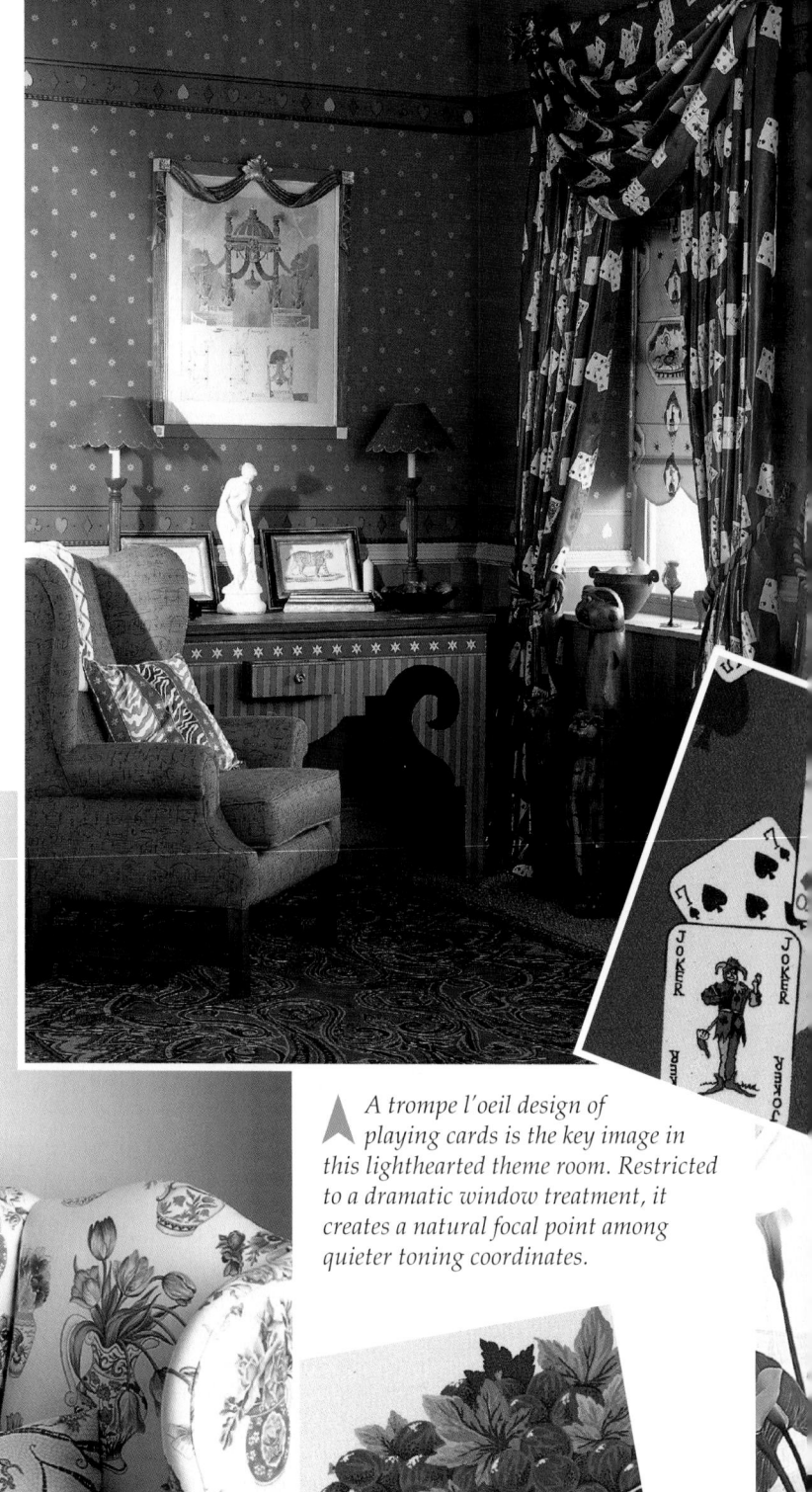

▲ A trompe l'oeil design of playing cards is the key image in this lighthearted theme room. Restricted to a dramatic window treatment, it creates a natural focal point among quieter toning coordinates.

◄ Beautifully illustrated studies of fine porcelain are almost as exquisite as the real thing. Fascinating in their own right, these prints of flower-filled jugs and cups and saucers take on an extra dimension as chair and screen covers.

A collection of antique clocks makes an amusing subject for a furnishing print and wall border, in a setting where period style blends easily with simple, modern lines.

Botanical studies are usually viewed behind glass or in a book, but as a unique furnishing design they are startlingly effective – fabric paints and a steady hand are all you need.

La feuille dont la plus grande largeur est au milieu, est plus régulière, avec un nombre plus grand de lobes (7 à 8) et les nervures latérales ne se prolongent pas jusqu'au bout des lobes ni jusqu'au cre-

CLASSICAL IMAGES

The graceful lines of classical architecture – the sinuous lines of columns and design reliefs from ancient facades – have become increasingly popular as black-and-white design images on fabrics and wallcoverings. Their tremendous visual impact is particularly striking in clean-lined schemes with other black-and-white details, such as checkered tiles, stripes and checks. Classical images look best in dramatic settings – with sumptuous drapes and an abundance of gilt – and as focal point furnishings in neutral contemporary schemes, where they team well with iron and steel. They also look stunning with accent colors – mauve, aqua or acid yellow all underline a graphic, modern look, while deep crimson, emerald green or deepest sky blue suggest a period feel.

You can capture the look with a photocopier; enlarge or reduce copies of old engravings and borders, or choose from one of the specialist groupings of preselected Print Room designs and ornamental borders. Paste the designs to walls or screens in the traditional Georgian manner; create panels, a dado or picture rail, or customize a piece of furniture with a classical decoupage design.

Less is more when it comes to using strong graphic images. The success of this scheme, where the blind with its classical column print is the focus of attention, owes much to its simplicity – and style.

The effect is bold and theatrical, in a hall where a design of classical vases creates a dramatic frame for a narrow hallway, and the dark lines of a designer chair complement the graphic prints.

EASTERN INFLUENCES

All the sumptuous patterns and exotic colors of the ancient spice routes have found their way into our decorative heritage – their earthy richness and vibrant glow inspire many modern schemes.

◄ Based on the exotic qualities and rich color palette of Indian textiles, this modern range of coordinating designs draws on the intricate detailing of a traditional decorative style for inspiration.

The sumptuous patterns of the East have had a lasting influence on western design – from the swirling, sinuous patterns of traditional paisley, based on the exotic, spice-colored fabrics imported from India in the 18th century, to the geometric precision of tribal rug patterns from the Middle East.

In an ever-shrinking world, where improved communications and easy travel bring global influences into everyday life so readily, it is perfectly logical that the colors and designs of other cultures should become more familiar and accessible than in the past. Eastern influences, with their jewel-like hues and intricate patterns associated with the textiles and artefacts found along the old trade routes, are particular favorites. They are easily recognizable in decorating and furniture stores everywhere, both as original imports, and as the inspiration and starting points for more home-grown design looks, on wallcoverings and borders, fabrics, accessories and fittings.

INDIAN INFLUENCES

The distinctive teardrop or flower-filled cone 'paisley' shape, is an enduring eastern motif which finds its way into many western designs, both as itself and in elaborate variations. It is named after the Scottish town of that name where, during the 19th century, beautifully patterned woolen shawls were produced, taking their inspiration from the designs on Indian silks.

The original paisley design draws on traditional Indian folklore and myth, flowering shrubs, lotus leaves and mango flower buds, all surrounded by intricate geometric fill-in backgrounds. At first glance, the colors in traditional paisley patterns seem to merge together, but a closer inspection reveals a rich, closely packed mix of different colors. This can be a useful tool in interior decoration, where you can pick out single colors to use as accents and highlights. Many modern paisley-inspired designs take the main motifs and work them against plainer, clear-colored backgrounds, or incorporate them into bands and stripes.

Soft muted reds and rich ochres – the dusty earth colors of India – provide a warming balance in a pale neutral bedroom. The traditional paisley shawl, used as a bed throw, adds subtle pattern interest and the inspiration for color accents throughout the scheme.

The glowing colors and vibrant contrasts of Indian silks inspire the color scheme and give this sitting room a definite Indian influence. The stylized patterns on the curtains and sofa both echo traditional paisley motifs, while dark wood furniture, an intricate metal chandelier and handcrafted accessories add authentic-looking style details.

Diverse looks

Distinctive embroidery from the Indian continent – crewelwork from Kashmir, brilliant, mirrored work from Rajasthan, appliqué and patchwork from Gujarat, as well as many other regional styles – have also found their way into western decorative style. The rich, jewel-bright colors work well with dark furniture and also as highlights in neutral schemes. These embroidered fabrics also adapt easily, moving from a wholly 'ethnic' look to blend in with more contemporary styles and schemes. One trick is to take a color from the work to use as a background setting or main accent. Brilliantly colored saris make impressive – and relatively inexpensive – window and bed drapes, and block-printed Indian cotton bedspreads can also serve as tablecloths and throws.

The textures of Indian textiles and artefacts also have an important influence. Soft white Indian cottons with their thick, nubby surfaces and loose weave, and muslin-fine, smooth cottons have become a mainstay of many modern neutral/natural schemes. Rough-hewn and carved wood, and chunky woven baskets with smooth, shiny brass trims also provide surface interest in room settings far removed from their origins.

▲ Indian crewelwork fabrics have a distinctive creamy-white background, and the softly colored yarns used to embroider the designs blend easily with many western schemes. In this dining room they make attractive curtains, while a typically patterned Indian bedspread becomes a complementary tablecloth.

◄ Shades of red ochre have strong associations with Indian design, and in decorating terms, their rich but muted tones add a welcome warming touch to cooler climes. These paisley-inspired coordinates are shown to advantage against warm-toned neutrals and dark, Indian-inspired furniture. Carefully chosen accessories such as the elephant pictures, teak chest and brass lantern help to underline the eastern influence.

137

MIDDLE EASTERN INFLUENCES

The unmistakable diamond shapes and rich earthy reds and crimsons of kilim rugs are probably the most easily recognizable of Middle Eastern patterns. A design classic in western homes, these rugs suit traditional furnishings and styles as well as relaxed, contemporary looks, where they contrast comfortably with stripped pine, light woods and pale neutrals. Originally made by the nomadic tribes from Persia and Turkey, these covetable, pileless rugs used fine quality wools to allow for frequent folding. Kilim-inspired prints abound on upholstery fabrics, and you can often find pillow and stool covers made from rescued portions of damaged kilims – or attractive modern copies. For a freer look, while retaining some of the formal charm of a traditional design, there are hand-knotted Gabbeh rugs from Iran, which depict scenes from everyday life in a colorful, spontaneous way. Their simple and naively figurative detailing looks particularly attractive in informal modern interiors.

Exotic spicy shades – yellow ochre, burnt sienna, raw and burnt umber, terra-cotta – are typical of the Middle East. With all the subtleties of natural dyes, these colors have a softness that makes them easy to assimilate into a scheme, where they create a warm and welcoming feeling. Try planning a color scheme on the gentle contrasts and glowing harmonies of the style, adding the typical details associated with the Middle East – Moorish arches, intricate brass filigree work, step-edged ziggurat patterns on tiles and borders – or simply opt for a few exotic details to use as accessories.

Eastern spices – in this case turmeric and ginger – inspire a spice route color scheme with contrasting blue. The paisley influence is apparent in the wallcovering and fabric prints, while the divan, piled pillows, tassel trims and handcrafted candle holders all hint at exotic Middle Eastern style.

◀ *Linked by color, East meets West with spicy red as the go-between. The exuberantly patterned kilim rug makes an impromptu bed hanging, while a toning pillow establishes the design style in what is otherwise a typically western scheme.*

▶ *The colors and patterns of these intricately detailed Turkish tiles demonstrate a traditional pattern format. These and similar designs have a clarity and rhythm that has been an inspiration to western decorators and designers for hundreds of years.*

◀ *Modern comforts and a traditional furnishing style are complemented by rich colors and subtle patterns from Turkey and the Middle East. The repetitive order of the fireplace tiles – hexagons and triangle filler-shapes – creates the star effects so familiar in Turkish and Middle Eastern design. As an outstanding feature, the tiles are balanced by the bold motifs on the rug and pillow.*

▲ *Tribal rugs, originally handwoven by the nomadic peoples of Persia, Turkey and the Middle East, make a unique statement, whether used singly or as a sumptuous collection. The rich but glowing colors owe their subtlety to traditional vegetable dyes, while the symbolic, stylized designs account for their perfectly balanced proportions.*

139

BLENDING STYLES

Eastern influences have made a lasting impression on modern home style. In many homes, fabrics and artifacts from very different sources sit happily together, linked by color and shape or a visual balance created by their contrasts. In the room below, a rich blue, familiar in Indian and Middle Eastern designs, is taken as a glowing color for the walls. The upholstery design takes inspiration from images in Indian painted miniatures, while the rug and many of the accessories come from farther afield. The room is essentially western, but the bold colors point to a more exotic starting point.

As accents, small details from one particular source can make quite an impact. For the best effect in an otherwise different room style, balance their presence with more than one item, to avoid any hint of being out of place. Accessories that earn their place include distinctive glass lanterns, brilliantly colored glassware, dark wood furniture, sumptuous silks and embroidered fabrics and, of course, patterned rugs.

▶ *Intricate tracery on this folding screen owes much to eastern pattern influences and style. Made from versatile MDF, similarly detailed panels and moldings are available from specialty mail order suppliers.*

◀ *Cozy throws have become a furnishing favorite in recent times. Pieced together like a quilt from more than one fabric design, throws are an ideal way to balance and coordinate different colors and patterns in the scheme – especially one with a global look.*

▼ *Anyone who loves living with vibrant color can take a lead from the eastern palette. Intense blue walls, exotic fabric prints, patterns and ethnic artifacts all bear the hallmark of eastern styles.*

▲ *Antique textiles such as these Indian embroideries have a muted glow that suits traditional schemes as well as many subtle contemporary looks. Color creates the necessary link, and here, warm tones, earthy terra-cotta and warm red blend together harmoniously.*

INDEX

Photograph Acknowledgments: Cover Creative Publishing international, 5-6 Creative Publishing international, 7 Creative Publishing international, 8-9(b) Decorwool, 9(t) Next Interiors, (br) Robert Harding Syndication/IPC Magazines/Country Homes & Interiors, 10 Robert Harding Syndication/ IPC Magazines/Ideal Home, 11 Abode Interiors, 12(t,br) Robert Harding Syndication/IPC Magazines/Homes & Gardens, (bl) Robert Harding Syndication/Homes & Ideas, 13 Elizabeth Whiting & Associates/Brian Harrison, 14(t) Elizabeth Whiting & Associates/ Neil Lorimer, (b) Abode Interiors, 15(t) Robert Harding Syndication/Ideal Home/Dominic Blackmore, (b) Robert Harding Syndication/Homes & Gardens/James Merrell, 16(t) Robert Harding Syndication/Homes & Gardens/Andreas von Einsiedel, (b) Robert Harding Syndication/Homes & Gardens/James Merrell, 17(t) Abode Interiors, (b) Worldwide Syndication, 18(t) Abode Interiors, (b) Robert Harding Syndication/Country Homes & Interiors/Christopher Drake, 19 Robert Harding Syndication/Country Homes & Interiors/Christopher Drake, 20(tr) Habitat UK, (b) Robert Harding Syndication/BBC Homes and Antiques/Brian Harrison, 21(r) BHS, (l) Robert Harding Syndication/Homes & Ideas/Dominic Blackmore, 22(t) Robert Harding Syndication/Woman & Home/Debi Treloar, (bl) Robert Harding Syndication/Options/Christopher Drake, (br) Eaglemoss/Graham Rae, 23(tl) Habitat UK, (tr) Elizabeth Whiting & Associates, (b) Elizabeth Whiting & Associates/Spike Powell, 24(tr) Robert Harding Syndication/Homes & Gardens/Michael Dunne, (cr) Robert Harding Syndication/Country Homes & Interiors/Bill Batten, (br) Robert Harding Syndication/Homes & Ideas/Dominic Blackmore, 25 Harlequin Fabrics, 26(tr) Robert Harding Syndication/Homes & Gardens/Nick Barlow, (bl) Robert Harding Syndication/Country Homes & Interiors/Fritz von der Schulenberg, 26-27(bc) Elizabeth Whiting & Associates/Peter Woloszynski, 27(tr) Elizabeth Whiting & Associates/Brian Harrison, (cr) Crowson Fabrics, 28(tc) Harlequin Fabrics, 28-29(c) Elizabeth Whiting & Associates/Nadia McKenzie, 28(bl) Osborne and Little, 29(tr) Robert Harding Syndication/Homes & Gardens/Tim Beddow, (br) Robert Harding Syndication/ Country Homes & Interiors/Simon Wheeler, 30(tr) Sanderson, (cl) Elizabeth Whiting & Associates/Brian Harrison, (br) Biggie Best, 31 Elizabeth Whiting & Associates/Neil Lorimer, 32-33(t) Ariadne Holland, 33(b) Elizabeth Whiting & Associates/Spike Powell, 34(tl) Laura Ashley, (b) Crown Wallcoverings, 35(t) Robert Harding Syndication/Country Homes & Interiors/ Christopher Drake, (b) Creative Publishing international, 36(tr) Elizabeth Whiting & Associates/Dennis Stone, (bl) Dulux, (br) BHS, 37 Robert Harding Syndication/Homes & Gardens/Trevor Richards, 38(t) Elizabeth Whiting & Associates/Tommy Candler, (c) Elizabeth Whiting & Associates/Tim Beddow, (bl) Elizabeth Whiting & Associates/Di Lewis, (br) Robert Harding Picture Library, 39(t) Elizabeth Whiting & Associates/Spike Powell, (bl) Elizabeth Whiting & Associates/Dominic Whiting, (br) Elizabeth Whiting & Associates/Di Lewis, 40(t) Elizabeth Whiting & Associates/Tim Beddow, (bl) Elizabeth Whiting & Associates/Michael Dunne, (br) Ariadne Holland, 41(tr) Elizabeth Whiting & Associates/Ian Parry, 42(t,c) Robert Harding Picture Library, (bl) Images Colour Library, (br) Elizabeth Whiting & Associates/ Nadia McKenzie, 43-44 Creative Publishing international, 45 Marie Claire Idées/Chabaneix, 46(tl) Eaglemoss/Graham Rae, (tr) Elizabeth Whiting & Associates/Jean-Paul Bonhommet, (b) Crown Wallcoverings, 47(tl) Ariadne Holland, (tr) Eaglemoss/Graham Rae, (b) Elizabeth Whiting & Associates/Steve Hawkins, 48(t) Crown Paints, (bl) Elizabeth Whiting & Associates/ Spike Powell, (br) Eaglemoss/Graham Rae, 49(tl) Robert Harding Syndication/Ideal Home/Lucinda Symons, (tr) Eaglemoss/Graham Rae, (b) Ariadne Holland, 50(tr) Robert Harding Syndication/Country Homes & Interiors/Tom Leighton, (c) Elizabeth Whiting & Associates/Di Lewis, (b) Worldwide Syndication, (br) Sanderson, 51 Home Flair Magazine, 52(tl) Eaglemoss/ Graham Rae, (tr) Doe Het Zelf Holland, (bl) Robert Harding Syndication/IPC Magazines/Homes & Gardens, 53(tl,cr) Robert Harding Syndication/Homes & Ideas/Dominic Blackmore, (bl) Eaglemoss/Graham Rae, (br) The Stencil Store, 54(tr) Elizabeth Whiting & Associates/Peter Woloszynski, (cr) Eaglemoss/Graham Rae, (bl) Elizabeth Whiting & Associates/Andreas von Einsiedel, 55(tr) Robert Harding Syndication/Homes & Gardens/Jan Baldwin, (bl) Sanderson, 56(tr) Robert Harding Syndication/Options/James Merrell, (bl) Elizabeth Whiting & Associates/Dennis Stone, (br) Laura Ashley, 57 Robert Harding Syndication/Homes & Ideas/Russell Sadur, 58(tr) Robert Harding Syndication/Homes & Ideas/Bill Reavell, (bl) Laura Ashley, (br) Eaglemoss/Lizzie Orme, 59(tl) Robert Harding Syndication/Ideal Home/Nadia McKenzie, (tr) Eaglemoss/Lizzie Orme, (br) Robert Harding Syndication/Homes & Gardens/ Polly Wreford, 60(tl) Eaglemoss/Lizzie Orme, (tr) Laura Ashley, (bl) Elizabeth Whiting & Associates/Ian Parry, 61(tr) Elizabeth Whiting & Associates/Brian Harrison, (c) Eaglemoss/Lizzie Orme, (b) Elizabeth Whiting & Associates/Andreas von Einsiedel, 62(tr) Robert Harding Syndication/Country Homes & Interiors/Christopher Drake, (cl) Dulux, (cr) The Pier, (bl) The Stencil Store, 63(t) Ariadne Holland, (br) Robert Harding Syndication/Homes & Gardens/Trevor Richards, 64(br) Robert Harding Syndication/Homes & Ideas/Colin Poole, 64-65(t) Ariadne Holland, 65(b) Robert Harding Syndication/Ideal Home/Graham Rae, 66(tl) Elizabeth Whiting & Associates/Michael Dunne, (tr) Home Flair Magazine, (b) Robert Harding Syndication/Homes & Gardens/Simon Brown, 67(t) Dulux, (bl) Robert Harding Syndication/Homes & Gardens/Simon Brown, (br) Robert Harding Syndication/Homes & Gardens/ Simon Upton, 68(tr) Elizabeth Whiting & Associates/Spike Powell, (bl) Next Interiors, (br) Robert Harding Syndication/Ideal Home/Dominic Blackmore, 69 Creative Publishing international, 70(tr) Worldwide Syndication, (b) Robert Harding Syndication/Country Homes & Interiors/Jan Baldwin, 71(t) Abode Interiors, 72(tl) Robert Harding Syndication/Homes & Gardens/Trevor Richards, (bl) Elizabeth Whiting & Associates/Jean-Paul Bonhommet, (br) Dulux, 73(tr) Robert Harding Syndication/Homes & Gardens/Tom Leighton, (br) Robert Harding Syndication/Woman & Home/Pia Tryde, 74(tr) Robert Harding Syndication/Homes & Gardens/Trevor Richards, (bl) Creative Publishing international, (br) Robert Harding Syndication/Homes & Ideas/Dominic Blackmore, 75 Elizabeth Whiting & Associates/Nick Carter, 76(bl) Vymura, 76-77 International Interiors, 77(bl) Abode Interiors, (br) Elizabeth Whiting & Associates/Tom Leighton, 78(tr) Fired Earth, (bl) Elizabeth Whiting & Associates/Dennis Stone, 79(t) Robert Harding Syndication/Country Homes & Interiors/Simon Brown, (br) Abode Interiors, 80(tr) Creative Publishing international, (cl) Abode Interiors, (cr) Robert Harding Syndication/Ideal Home/Graham Rae, (bl) G.P.& J Baker, 81, 82 Dulux, 83(tl,cr,br) Fired Earth, (bl) Elizabeth Whiting & Associates/Simon Upton, 84-85(t) Elizabeth Whiting & Associates/Tim Beddow, 84(bl) Robert Harding Syndication/Options/Tom Leighton, (br) Robert Harding Syndication/Homes & Ideas/Dominic Blackmore, 85(tr) Elizabeth Whiting & Associates, (br) Sanderson, 86(tr) Elizabeth Whiting & Associates, (cl) Dulux, (br) Robert Harding Syndication/Homes & Gardens/James Merrell, 87 Robert Harding Syndication/Brad Simmons Photography, 88(cr) Robert Harding Syndication/Brad Simmons Photography, (bl) Robert Harding Syndication/Country Homes & Interiors/Jan Baldwin, 89(tr) Elizabeth Whiting & Associates/Rodney Hyett, (br) Robert Harding Syndication/Brad Simmons Photography, 90(bl) Robert Harding Syndication/Brad Simmons Photography, 91(tl) Robert Harding Syndication/Brad Simmons Photography, (bl) Elizabeth Whiting & Associates/Brian Harrison, (br) Eaglemoss/Graham Rae, 92(tr,cl) Elizabeth Whiting & Associates/Nick Carter, (br) Eaglemoss/Graham Rae, 93(tc) Robert Harding Syndication/Homes & Gardens/Kiloran Howard, (sp) Eaglemoss/Graham Rae, 94(tl) Elizabeth Whiting & Associates, (bl) Eaglemoss/Graham Rae, (br) Robert Harding Syndication/Options/Jan Baldwin, 95(tl) Eaglemoss/Graham Rae, (b) Abode Interiors, (br) Elizabeth Whiting & Associates/Dennis Stone, 96(tr) Elizabeth Whiting & Associates/Peter Aprahamian, (cl) Eaglemoss/Graham Rae, (b) Robert Harding Syndication/Ideal Home/Graham Rae, (r) Eaglemoss/Graham Rae, 97(tl) Eaglemoss/Graham Rae, (tr) Elizabeth Whiting & Associates, (bl) Harlequin, (br) Eaglemoss/Graham Rae, 98(tl) Eaglemoss/Graham Rae, (tr) Robert Harding Syndication/Homes & Gardens/Trevor Richards, (cl) Elizabeth Whiting & Associates, (cr,bl) Eaglemoss/Graham Rae, (br) Elizabeth Whiting & Associates/Neil Lorimer, 99-100 Creative Publishing international, 101 Crowson Fabrics, 102(tl) Robert Harding Syndication/Homes & Gardens/Simon Brown, (tr) Laura Ashley, (b) Crowson Fabrics, 103(br) Sanderson, (l) Laura Ashley, (r) Textra, 104(tr,bl) Ceil Decor, 105(t) Boras, (b) Robert Harding Syndication/Homes & Ideas/Ian Skelton, 106-107(tc) Robert Harding Syndication/Homes & Gardens/Polly Wreford, 106(bl) Boras, 107(bl) Sanderson, (br) Robert Harding Syndication/Homes & Ideas/Bill Reavell, 108(tc,tr,c,bl) Robert Harding Syndication/Homes & Ideas/Dominic Blackmore, (br) Abode Interiors, 109(tl) Robert Harding Syndication, (br) Robert Harding Syndication/Homes & Ideas/Dominic Blackmore, 110(tr) Robert Harding Syndication/Homes & Ideas/Dominic Blackmore, (cl) Robert Harding Syndication/Ideal Home, (bl) Elizabeth Whiting & Associates/Steve Hawkins, (br) Robert Harding Syndication/Homes & Ideas/Dominic Blackmore, 111 Robert Harding Syndication/Homes & Ideas/Dominic Blackmore, 112(b) Robert Harding Syndication/Homes & Ideas/Flavio Gallozzi, 112-113(b) Robert Harding Syndication/Homes & Ideas/Dominic Blackmore, 113(tr,bl) Marie Claire Idées/Becquet/Faure, (br) Elizabeth Whiting & Associates/Mark Luscombe-Whyte, 114(t) Robert Harding Syndication/Homes & Gardens/Owen Walker, (cl) Robert Harding Syndication/Homes & Ideas/Bill Reavell, (cr) Robert Harding Syndication/Homes & Ideas/Dominic Blackmore, (b) Robert Harding Syndication/Ideal Home/Ian Skelton, 115 Elizabeth Whiting & Associates/Spike Powell, 116(tl) Ariadne Holland, (tr) Eaglemoss/Lizzie Orme, (b) Textra, 117(tl) Robert Harding Syndication/Ideal Home/Graham Rae, (br) Elizabeth Whiting & Associates/Brian Harrison, 118(tl) Eaglemoss/Lizzie Orme, (tr) Elizabeth Whiting & Associates/Di Lewis, (b) Anna French, 119(t) Coloroll, (c) Robert Harding Syndication/Homes & Ideas/Dominic Blackmore, (b) BHS, 120(tr) Dulux, (cl) Laura Ashley, (bl) Robert Harding Syndication/Ideal Home/ Nadia McKenzie, (br) Worldwide Syndication, 121 Robert Harding Syndication/Homes & Gardens/Polly Wreford, 122-123 Robert Harding Syndication/Homes & Ideas/Dominic Blackmore, 122(t) Eaglemoss, (br) Sofa Workshop Direct, 123(br) Robert Harding Syndication/Woman & Home/Steven Dalton, (br) Robert Harding Syndication/Homes & Gardens/Polly Wreford, 124(tr) Next Interiors, (bl) Anna French, (br) Harlequin Fabrics, 125(tr) Harlequin Fabrics, (br) Eaglemoss/Simon Page-Ritchie, 126(tr) Robert Harding Syndication/Ideal Home/Lucinda Symons, (cr) Mail Order Sofa Co, (bl) Next Interiors, (br) Robert Harding Syndication/Homes & Ideas, 127 Robert Harding Syndication/Ideal Home/Dominic Blackmore, 128(tr) Robert Harding Syndication/Homes & Gardens/Henry Bourne, (bl) Robert Harding Syndication/Homes & Gardens/Hannah Lewis, (br) Robert Harding Syndication/Homes & Gardens/Henry Bourne, 129(tl) Robert Harding Syndication/Homes & Ideas/Dominic Blackmore, (tr) Elizabeth Whiting & Associates/Brian Harrison, (br) Robert Harding Syndication/Country Homes & Interiors, 130(tr) Abode Interiors, (bl) Elizabeth Whiting & Associates/Brian Harrison, (br) Robert Harding Syndication/Homes & Gardens/Kiloran Howard, 131 Elizabeth Whiting & Associates/Di Lewis, 132(tr) Romo Ltd, (bl) Robert Harding Syndication/Country Homes & Interiors/Polly Wreford, (br) Marie Claire Idées/Chabaneix, 133 Warner Fabrics, 134(tr) Elizabeth Whiting & Associates/Nick Carter, (bl) Elizabeth Whiting & Associates/Tim Beddow, (br) Robert Harding Syndication/Homes & Ideas/Dominic Blackmore, 135 Harlequin Fabrics, 136(tr) Robert Harding Syndication/Homes & Gardens/Polly Wreford, (cl) Harlequin Fabrics, (br) Dorma, 137 Elizabeth Whiting & Associates, 138(tr) Fired Earth, (b) Romo Ltd, 139 Fired Earth, 140(tr) Jali Ltd, (cl) The Interior Archive/Simon Brown, (c) Dorma, (b) Robert Harding Syndication/Ideal Home/Lucinda Symons.

Creative Publishing international offers a variety of how-to books. For information write:

Creative Publishing international
Subscriber Books
5900 Green Oak Drive
Minnetonka, MN 55343
1-800-328-3895